ALTERED ART CIRCUS!

QUARRY

TECHNIQUES FOR JOURNALS, PAPER DOLLS, ART CARDS, AND ASSEMBLAGES

Altered Art Circus!

BEVERLY MASSACHUSETTS

QUARRY BOOKS

LISA KETTELL

First published in the United States of America by
Quarry Books, a member of
Quayside Publishing Group
100 Cummings Center
Suite 406-L
Beverly, Massachusetts 01915-6101
Telephone: (978) 282-9590
Fax: (978) 283-2742
www.quarrybooks.com

Library of Congress Cataloging-in-Publication Data
Kettell, Lisa.
    Altered Art Circus! : altering techniques, art cards, and other magical projects /
Lisa Kettell.
        p. cm.
ISBN 978-1-59253-487-6
1. Handicraft. 2. Fancy work. I. Title.

TT857.K47 2009
745.5--dc22   2008022606
                                         CIP

Design: bradhamdesign.com
Photography by Lexi Boeger with the exception of pages 111–128; some background and
accent images from www.istockphoto.com.
Technical Edit: Marla Stefanelli

Printed in Singapore

PHOTO POST CARD

ADDRESS

UNITED STATES

C O N T E N T S

INTRODUCTION
8

 I N T R O D

*E*VER SINCE I COULD HOLD A CRAYON I HAVE CREATED A FANTASY WORLD.

Inspiration came from savoring every last detail from fairytales and short stories such as *Peter Pan* and *Alice in Wonderland*. On Sundays, my grandfather would take me to his parent's house for crumb cake and breakfast goodies. My great-aunts and -uncles would sit at the table and talk about the good old days as I watched my great grand-father walk around the property as if he were hunting for treasure. Because he owned a salvage yard, exploring was second nature to him—a trait that was passed on to me. (Coincidentally, we share the same birth date.)

As time passed, my passion expanded to illustration. I tried to get my hands on every comic or picture book I could find and began teaching myself how to draw the characters. Both my grandmother and uncle are illustrators and have their own style, but I was struggling to find mine. A big question in my mind was: How do you pick a specific style or art form when you like everything you see? I've come to the conclusion that you don't pick. You explore inspiration from all art forms, and eventually you'll discover your niche.

As a self-taught artist, I am always looking for ways to challenge my creativity, which has led me to explore the world of digital illustration and altered design. I have also been quite inspired by the History Channel, another big influence on my work. In addition, research on the Internet has led me to information, inspiration, creative blogs, and art groups where I have made many friends. I created *The Faerie Zine*, a publication that is filled with amazing works of art, project ideas, samples, collage sheets, stories, interesting facts, and my own art—and from that sprang this book.

My goal is to bring altered art to a new level by combining novel techniques, materials, and projects. You will find art recipes made from household items, garden and hardware supplies, and children's art-and-craft materials. You will integrate unique ephemera into exciting two- and three-dimensional projects.

Don't be afraid to experiment. This book is about playtime for grown-ups. We all have our daily commitments and schedules, which can cause chaos or stress in our lives. When we finally do find the time for art, we can suffer a creative block or loss of inspiration, making it very challenging to create a new piece and figure out what techniques to apply. This is when inspiration is a key. This is the time to visit the *Altered Art Circus!*

To get there you will need a map and a key, which can be found in the following pages. Escape into fantasy—daydream of chocolate fountains or flying cupcakes, wear a pixie tiara, visit the fairy opera, or step inside an apothecary shop. Take these artifacts and embark on your own journey—you may never want to come back.

I want to bring you—the reader, the daydreamer, the explorer, the artist—to a place you have never been before—a place where you can unleash your creative muse and explore hidden worlds. I hope to lead you down new artistic paths and illuminate your life.

Whether your creative time is spent treasure hunting for new ideas and supplies in your home, at the antique market, or in a bookstore, remember one thing—after reading this book, you can journey fearlessly into your own imagination filled with magical follies and pure delight.

—LISA KETTELL

veling Bumbelina's

CHAPTER ONE

GETTING STARTED

Before you start any project in this book,
you must understand some essentials:

✪ ✪ ✪

BELIEVE IN YOURSELF!

When you believe in yourself, anything is possible.

✪ ✪ ✪

{ *Remember that* }
ONE MAN'S TRASH IS ANOTHER MAN'S TREASURE,

so keep your eyes open for unusual new materials.

✪ ✪ ✪

BEAUTY IS IN THE EYE OF THE BEHOLDER.

Create for yourself first. Make yourself smile.
Don't worry about the scrutiny of others.

✪ ✪ ✪

{ *Remember that* }
IMPERFECTIONS ARE OFTEN PRICELESS.

As you explore altered art you will find the grungier,
and more scratches, the better.

ARTISTIC INFLUENCES

THE PROJECTS IN THIS BOOK DRAW FROM MANY ART TRADITIONS. HERE IS AN OVERVIEW OF THE FEATURED TECHNIQUES AND ART STYLES.

Altered art is described as a form of mixed-media artwork that alters the appearance of an original form into something else.

The word collage comes from the French word *coller*, meaning to stick two pieces together, or to paste. Pablo Picasso used this term frequently at the beginning of the twentieth century. During this time, collage became a unique feature of modern art. Collage is characterized as an artistic composition made from various materials that are glued onto a surface.

Découpage is the art of gluing cutout pictures onto an object for decorative purposes. When complete, the object is coated with several layers of sealant for protection.

Digital collage is the process of using computer image-editing software to create a collage.

Mixed-media is the term used to describe a variety of materials. It is the creation of artwork where more than one medium has been employed.

Photomontage is a collage made from photographs. It is the process of making a composite picture by cutting and masking a number of photographs, which are placed on photographic plates. Sometimes the composite picture is photographed so the final image is converted back into a single photographic print. The modern way to achieve this effect is through computer image-editing software.

COPYRIGHT AND COLLAGE

Copyright violation is the unauthorized use of material that is protected by a copyright. It is a violation when another party reproduces a piece in some form or another without consent of the original copyright holder.

If you are an artist who enjoys working in collage, you need to be aware of copyright issues, particularly if you intend to sell or profit from your work.

A safe approach is to work with antique art from the early 1900s, family photographs, and ephemera. Visit the website of the United States Library of Congress at www.loc.gov for additional information on copyright issues.

The Victorians were famous for creating the odd and comical postcards that feature large heads placed on top of different bodies or creatures. They were lovers of fantasy and created artwork revolving around their passion for anything unusual.

TOOLS AND SUPPLIES

TO GET STARTED

Start collecting decorative materials such as the papers, fabrics, and embellishments. It is also good to have an assortment of paints and drawing materials on hand. Assemble this basic tool kit and keep it handy to complete most of the projects in this book.

PAPER MATERIALS

Collect vintage images, scrapbook paper, poster board, cardstock, matte board, ephemera, and memorabilia. Look for carnival, circus, or movie-ticket stubs, theatre programs, dance cards, cabinet cards, vintage doctor and business receipts, vintage paper patterns, dress-form measuring tapes, retro advertisements, vintage toy catalogs, dictionaries, newspapers, and wallpaper.

SHARED IMAGERY

In the back of the book, beginning on page 111, you will find a sampling of the images used in the projects as well as additional art and photographs that you can use for your own creations. Make color photocopies, and enlarge or reduce them as you desire. You can also use this gallery as inspiration to search for unique images of your own.

FABRICS AND EMBELLISHMENTS

For interesting fabrics explore old draperies, napkins, tablecloths, vintage clothing, old ball gowns, crinoline, and doll clothes. Broken jewelry, rhinestones, sequins, beaded-fabric scraps, wedding embellishments, berry picks, ornaments, ribbon, tinsel, garland, and chenille strips are great embellishments. Model Magic modeling material air dries to cure and is used to sculpt shapes and create small embellishments. And don't forget glitter glue, glitter-glue pens, three-dimensional paint, and puffy-paint pens.

BASIC TOOL KIT

★ scissors
★ decorative scissors
★ hole punch
★ wire pliers
★ brayer or rolling pin
★ hot-glue gun
★ small screwdriver
★ paintbrushes
★ foam brushes
★ X-acto or craft knife

Unfinished Bases and Forms

Consider small wooden doll cabinets, wardrobe closets, doll furniture, frames, wooden and cardboard cigar boxes, blocks of wood, tassels, doll kits, doll forms, rubber-toy animals, glass bulbs, canning jars, and vegetable tins as a foundation for a project.

Paints, Inks, and Drawing Media

Acrylic paints, oil paints, gesso, inks, and watercolors are essential supplies. I recommend the following:

★ Buy a variety of acrylic paint, available in small plastic bottles, in black, brown, white, cream, yellow, pink, red, purple, blue, light blue, and light green. These wash up with water.

★ Gesso is white and used as a base-coat primer. Use gesso as a primer for hard-to-paint surfaces so subsequent coats of paint will adhere. Gesso is also the perfect base coat for craft foam. It will cause the surface to stiffen and gives the foam a woodlike strength.

★ Oil paints and water-soluble oil paints have a wonderful consistency. They also have a longer drying time than acrylics, leaving more time to mix colors. These paints work best over beeswax or crayon.

★ Inks are used with rubber stamps and work extremely well as a wood stain. The ink seeps into the wood and accents the grain.

★ Ink pens, paint pens, and gel pens add fine-line details to your artwork and can be combined with other mediums.

★ Cray pods, oil pencils, and watercolor pencils can be blended together for additional artistic effects.

Glues, Finishes, and Transfer Mediums

★ Basic white glue

★ Modge Podge Matte-mat

Ephemera

Ephemera is referred to as printed material. It comes from a Greek reference meaning, things lasting no more than one day. Some ideal collectible ephemera are cigarette cards and labels, greeting cards, vintage apothecary receipts, advertising-trade cards, baseball cards, tickets, and letters!

★ Acrylic matte-gel medium works perfectly for gluing paper to paper, and photographs to paper, wood, metal, glass, and fabric. Apply the medium with a foam brush.

★ Use tacky glue for adhering lightweight objects to a project. White glue is a fine substitute for tacky glue, it just takes longer to dry.

★ For extra hold use an industrial glue or epoxy, and follow the manufacturer's instructions.

★ Use acrylic-gel medium, wood stain, blender pens, Liquid Sculpey, and a heat tool for image transfers.

★ Acrylic crackle medium creates a weathered look for a vintage finish.

★ For a fast bond, use hot-glue. I do not recommend using hot-glue to adhere objects to metal or glass as it can easily break off.

Heat Tool, Embossing Gun, Melting Pot, and Rolling Pin

★ A heat tool can cut, emboss wood, carve gourds, burn paper edges, and transfer laser images to almost any surface except plastic.

★ An embossing tool heats pigment powders, shrinks shrink-film, and embosses on Friendly Plastic.

★ A mini quilting iron melts crayons and beeswax onto projects.

★ A craft melting pot melts ultra-embossing powder for glazing and stamping, and can also be used to dip or pour wax, glue, and more.

★ A rolling pin or brayer helps adhere glued papers together and removes any air bubbles.

Household and Hardware Supplies

Employ these common items in your work: white vinegar, bleach, liquid starch, borax, petroleum jelly, fingernail hardener, coffee, tea, salt, hot-cocoa mix, food coloring, grape juice, soda, flavored drink powders, vinyl spackle, wood putty, wood glue, Miracle Gro, masking tape, packaging tape, crayons, and old toys.

ℬASIC TECHNIQUES, TIPS, AND TRICKS

TECHNIQUES ARE DEVELOPED THROUGH EXPERIMENTATION AND ARE OFTEN DISCOVERED AS A RESULT OF MISSING AN ITEM OR TWO FOR A SPECIFIC PROJECT—THIS IS SERENDIPITY AT ITS BEST. LEARNING NEW TRICKS CAN PAVE THE PATH FOR NEW DEVELOPMENTS IN OUR ART.

COLLAGE METHODS

USING ADHESIVES

The most important part of a project is determining which glue to use. I recommend ordinary white glue or Modge Podge for basic collage. For assemblages and more detailed collage work use acrylic-gel matte. The bond and smoothness of this medium makes it the perfect companion for your work. It can also be used as a topcoat over glued or découpaged items or for photo transferring.

REINFORCE PAPER IMAGES

When an image needs to stand upright on its own, reinforce the image by adding a layer of poster board or cardstock, which stiffens the paper and makes it more durable. Cut out an image, use Modge Podge to glue it to the poster board, and then trim the poster board even with the image. For a three-dimensional image that will be seen from both sides, use two images (reverse one) and glue them to both sides of poster board.

SMOOTHING GLUED SURFACES

To eliminate air bubbles or crinkled paper, I recommend using a brayer or rolling pin. After gluing paper to poster board or a flat surface, roll the paper with a brayer or rolling pin. Then place the glued piece under a stack of books for an hour to dry. Another option for flattening a piece is to use an iron without steam. Heat the iron, place the glued piece under a piece of muslin fabric, and then iron flat.

Aging, Distressing, and Designer Finishes

Serendipity Polish

Aging a piece of work can be done in a variety of ways. One quick and easy way is to use shoe polish. You will need a brown-toned shoe polish and a soft cloth. Gently dab the cloth into the polish using your fingertips, and then lightly apply the polish to your artwork, adding thin layers until you reach the desired effect.

Tea, Coffee, and Cocoa Antiquing

What is more fun than aging a piece with tea, coffee, or cocoa? Everyone has these supplies around the house. First heat a pot of water and gather some cooking tweezers and foil pans. For tea staining, add three to four tea bags to the boiled water and let steep for two hours until the water is dark. Dip watercolor paper, ephemera, or fabric into the tea and let it soak for five minutes. Remove the item from the solution with tweezers and place on a flat surface to dry. To prevent paper from curling as it dries, place a few books over the paper when it is still slightly damp. Repeat as necessary to darken the effect.

For coffee and cocoa staining, substitute five tablespoons of either in the boiling water and follow the instructions above.

Fruit-Juice Dyeing

Fill a large pot with three cups of water, bring to a boil, and then add a 32-ounce (0.95 L) container of fruit juice, grape juice, or cranberry juice; stir. Slowly add one-third cup of rubbing alcohol. Boil for ten more minutes. Lower the temperature and stir for another ten minutes. Remove the pot from the heat and dip your paper, ephemera, or fabric into the pot to saturate it with the color. When satisfied with the color, remove with tweezers, and let dry.

Powder-Drink-Mix Dyeing

This uses the same technique as for juice dyeing. Substitute a packet of powder drink mix and follow the above instructions.

Walnut Ink and Ink Crystals

Much like coffee, tea, or cocoa staining, distressing inks can be purchased in a variety of colors from art or craft stores. The inks are sold in various forms: stamp pads, powders, and crystals. Follow the manufacturer's instructions.

Crackle Medium and Glazing

Crackle medium is easy to use and offers rewarding results when aging a project. Begin by painting your piece with a thick coat of a darker-tone color and let dry. Apply a generous amount of crackle medium and let it dry until the surface is slightly tacky. Finally, apply a lighter paint color over the crackle medium. When dry, you will see the paint crackle into unique random lines. For additional aging, apply a glazing medium over the piece.

Miracle Distress

Miracle Gro is an unexpected product to use for aging metal. The result is a distressed patina on metal, tin, and copper. Pour one cup of all-purpose Miracle Gro plant food into a bowl, and then slowly add water and stir to make a thick paste. Place the piece of metal, tin, or copper on a foil tray, and use an old paintbrush to paint the metal with the mixture; let dry. Continue applying the solution to the piece until the desired patina is achieved. The longer you leave the solution on, the more turquoise the patina will be.

Mud-Pie Grunge

To make a murky chocolate aging glaze, combine one part Modge Podge with two parts of chocolate-colored acrylic paint in a plastic disposable bowl; stir until you get a mud color. For a darker blend, add some dark-brown paint. For a sweet, decadent cupcake effect, use pink paint instead of brown.

Use this solution to paint on glass, metal, or wooden boxes. Sprinkle the painted piece with some sand, seeds, peanut shards, glitter, ceiling glitter flakes, or German-glass glitter to add texture.

Bleach and Salt Dying

Household bleach will add lighter specs of color to dark papers and fabric and add interest to tea- or coffee-stained items. Work in a well-ventilated area, and protect your skin, eyes, and the work surface. Place the piece in a foil pan. Wearing rubber gloves, fill a discarded turkey baster or syringe with bleach, and slowly drip it onto the piece. Try adding a few drops of food color, ink, or salt to the bleach, which will yield a variety of results. Let your project dry completely.

Embossing Tool

An embossing tool is used with pigment ink and embossing powder. The tool blows hot air to melt the embossing power. To make a rubber-stamp image, press the pigment ink-pad onto the rubber stamp, then turn the stamp over and press it onto the surface of choice. Immediately sprinkle embossing powder, or embossing glitter-powder, onto the still wet stamped image; gently shake off the excess. Move your heat tool in a circular motion over the stamped image until the powder melts and creates a raised surface.

Heat-Tool Transfers

For color or black-and-white copy transfers you will need a copy of an image from a laser printer. If you don't own a laser printer, copy the image with a laser copier. The surface you transfer to can be paper, fabric, wood, metal—anything but plastic. Place the copied image face down onto the transfer surface, tape or hold it in place, and then slowly rub the tip of the heat tool around your image in a continuous circular motion. Completely rub each small area at a time until the whole image has transferred.

For letter and word transfers, be sure to reverse the lettering using image-editing software on your computer before printing or copying it to create the laser print. If you don't have a laser printer, take your disk of image files to an office-supply copy center and print them out (ask for assistance if needed).

Acrylic-Gel-Medium Transfers

Choose an image that you want to transfer to another surface. Make a color or black-and-white copy of it on a laser printer or copier. Use a foam brush to coat the front of the image with gloss or matte acrylic-gel medium. Place the image face down onto the transfer surface and press down firmly. Smooth the image with a rolling pin, and wait a few minutes for it to dry. Then begin at a corner and peel back the paper just a bit. If the image hasn't completely transferred, then the image is still wet. Let it dry a bit longer, and then remove the paper. To remove any leftover paper residue, fill a small cup with water, dip your fingers in the water, and then gently rub off the residue with your moistened fingers.

Wood-Stain Pen or Blender-Pen Transfers

Start with a color or black-and-white laser copy of your image. Place the image face down on your surface of choice. Rub the back of the image with the wood-stain or blender pen, saturating the paper and until the image transfers. Let the paper dry for a few minutes, and then peel it off.

Packaging-Tape Transfers

Starting with a color or black-and-white laser copy of your image, place the image face down onto the sticky side of a piece of paper packaging tape. Use a rolling pin to press it smoothly onto the tape. Then place the taped image in a bowl of water and soak for two minutes. Remove it from the water, and begin peeling away the paper backing by rubbing with your fingers until all the paper is removed, and the image has transferred to the tape. The resulting image is transparent. Apply a layer of glue and attach the transfer to your project.

Cabinet Card

During the 1870s, photographs were usually mounted on cards measuring 4¼" x 6½" (10.8 x 16.5 cm), which had ornate lettering on the reverse side. The cards were mounted on the stiffer backing material due to the thinness of the photograph.

ALTERED ART CIRCUS!

CHAPTER TWO

DISCOVERED ARTIFACTS

✦ ✦ ✦

AS ARTISTS, WE ARE ALSO EXPLORERS

who love the thrill of finding forgotten treasures discarded
so many years ago, into which we can breathe a new life in the
form of our art. Even everyday items—old books, scraps
of wrapping paper—can become wonderful treasures.

✦ ✦ ✦

A DOLL HOUSE { *or storage case* }

can become an art book,

CIRCUS TOYS OR GARDEN PEAT POTS

make lovely treat containers and assemblages,

LEFTOVER PARTY HATS

make wonderful ornamental hats and dolls,

AND POKER CHIPS

become instant art coins and pendants.

There are so many artifacts waiting to be discovered.

{ All you need is a little inspiration. }

IN THE *Altered Art Circus!* YOU NEVER KNOW WHAT YOU WILL FIND LURKING BEHIND A CLOSED DOOR.

But one thing I do know—you will find magic
and mayhem hiding in Alistair's Closet of Mystery.
This project will lead you to search for magical supplies
such as tiny bottles, apothecary ephemera, and lots of glitter.

MATERIALS

* basic tool kit; see page 13
* two small wooden craft wall displays 7" wide x 8" tall (17.8 x 20.3 cm) (found in the wood section of craft stores)
* two small dollhouse-size glass bottles
* two brass hinges 1" x 1¾" (2.5 x 3 cm)
* paper (designer, handmade, wallpaper, tissue paper, etc.)
* poster board (large sheet)
* newspaper
* ribbon
* tinsel chenille stems
* vintage images, ephemera
* glitter and glitter-paint pens
* acrylic paint (black, brown, light blue, light green, white, cream)
* acrylic antique medium: brown
* glue: basic white glue, hot glue

Instructions for Alistair's Closet of Mystery

1. Paint the wooden wall displays with two coats of black acrylic paint; let dry between coats.

2. Line up the wall displays with the flat surfaces facing. Attach the hinges to the displays on one long side. Center each hinge on the side seam and screw the flaps in place on the displays.

3. Use white glue to adhere designer paper to the inside front of the assembled display. Cut a pocket from designer paper and glue the edges to the inside front over the designer paper.

4. Cut out a 6" x 24" (15.2 x 61 cm) strip of poster board. Accordion-fold the poster board into four 6" (15.2 cm) squares. Decorate the accordion-fold book by gluing newspaper to the inside pages. When dry, paint the pages with antique medium for an aged look. Glue an end square to the inside back display with hot-glue.

5. Add vintage images to the pages and cut a few extra to put in the front pocket. See pages 111–113 for possible image selections.

6. Create a smaller accordion book from a 4" (10.2 cm) -wide strip of poster board, fill with more images, wrap a ribbon around the book to close, and insert it into the front pocket.

7. Decorate the outside of the wall displays. Fill the two small glass bottles with glitter, cover with their lids, and randomly glue the bottles to the display. Embellish with a variety of glitter and paints. Wrap a ribbon around the displays to close.

SPELLBINDER'S ACADEMY IS THE PREMIER SCHOOL
FOR FINE YOUNG WITCHES AND IS LOCATED IN MAVENDER WOODS,
ROBINS COUNTY, ENGLAND.

{ *This book is dedicated to the school and its secrets.* }

For this project you will be making a vintage-style yearbook
from a medium-size scrapbook filled with papers, images,
and spellbinding techniques.

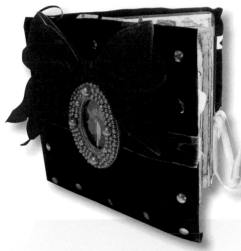

MATERIALS

- ★ basic tool kit; see page 13
- ★ medium-size scrapbook with removable pages
- ★ small oval frame
- ★ paper (designer, handmade, wallpaper, tissue paper, etc)
- ★ parchment paper
- ★ poster board (large sheet)
- ★ ribbon
- ★ black leather or vinyl
- ★ small brass upholstery tacks
- ★ tinsel chenille stems
- ★ vintage images, ephemera
- ★ glitter and glitter-paint pens
- ★ acrylic antique medium: brown
- ★ glue: basic white glue, industrial glue, hot-glue
- ★ colored oil pencils
- ★ other: rubber stamps, ink, chipboard letters, rhinestones, pearls, old keys, tags

INSTRUCTIONS FOR THE BOOK OF SECRETS

1. Open the scrapbook, and remove the screws from the adjustable page holder, take out the pages, saving one for a template.

2. Trace the page template onto ten pieces of parchment paper, and then cut the parchment paper to size. Line up the new pages with the template, mark the punched-hole locations, and then punch the holes. Insert the parchment pages into the scrapbook, and reassemble the page holder.

3. Embellish the pages with vintage cabinet cards and photographs. Glue each in place with white glue. When dry, color the images with colored oil pencils. If desired seal the colored images with a light coat of Modge Podge.

4. Create three paper pockets; one for the inside front cover, one for the inside back cover, and one for the back page. Use hot-glue to hold the pocket edges in place. Embellish the front inside cover with chipboard letters that spell "Faerie." Fill the pages with all types of fairy ephemera. Fill the back pockets with mermaid and travel ephemera.

5. Embellish the inside pages with more chipboard letters, ribbons, bookmarks, keys, tags, and a variety of glitter.

6. Decorate the outside of your book with leather borders cut 1" (2.5 cm) longer then the book edges. Secure the leather in place with upholstery tacks. Attach the small frame to the front cover with industrial glue. Cover the small frame with pearls. Tie a large wire-ribbon bow, and secure the bow above the frame with hot-glue.

Miss Anabelle Spellbinder

Anabelle is a direct ancestor of Merlinda Spellbinder, the founder of the Spellbinder School of Fine Witches. The key goal of the school is to teach young witches the fine art of magic, proper etiquette and the true meaning of being a witch. These values have earned the school its worldwide excellence and the number one title in the magic world.

Miss Maude Bellows

Maude has been the director of magic affairs at the school and works closely with Miss Spellbinder. Miss Bellows also teaches Potions one through five, Magic Leaf Reading and Phrenology.

GUIDE TO THE MER-PEOPLE

THE HOUSEWIFE KNOWS
MERMAID QUEEN SOAP
DO YOU?

TRAVEL MEMORIES

POCKET-POSIES

TUSSIE MUSSIES, THE INSPIRATION FOR THIS PROJECT, HAVE EXISTED IN SOME FORM SINCE MEDIEVAL TIMES.

MATERIALS

★ basic tool kit; see page 13

★ 12" (30.5 cm) square of poster board

★ peat pots (available at most garden supply centers)

★ decorative paper (designer, handmade, wallpaper, tissue, crepe paper, etc)

★ ribbons and trims

★ rhinestone button

★ broken necklace

★ vintage images, ephemera

★ 12" (30.5 cm) length of craft wire

★ Model Magic modeling material

★ glitter and glitter-paint pens

★ acrylic paint (black, brown, light blue, light green, pink, cream, gold)

★ crackle medium

★ glue: Modge Podge, Elmer's Gel Glue, hot-glue

These small flower bouquets, wrapped with moss or herbs, were worn or carried to mask the smells of the time. The Victorians, who were obsessed with flowers and horticulture, perfected the art of tussie mussies. Their versions of these flower cones, or posy holders, become quite ornate and were available in a multitude of styles.

In this project I have updated the classic version of the tussie mussie with the use of paper cones, peat pots, images, and a variety of embellishments. These tussie mussies, which I call pocket posies, are shown in a variety of styles and can be filled with items of your choice.

INSTRUCTIONS FOR THE CONE-SHAPED POCKET POSY

1. Enlarge the cone pattern on page 116, if desired. Apply Modge Podge to the poster board with a foam brush. Position the decorative paper of your choice on the poster board and press in place. Use a rolling pin to roll out any bubbles. Before the Modge Podge dries completely, shape the poster board into a cone with the decorative paper on the outside, and then hot-glue the edges of the cone in place.

2. Punch two holes in the cone on opposite sides of the upper edge. For the handle, thread ribbon through the two holes and tie a knot at each end to secure.

3. Embellish your cone with ribbon, decorative trim, jewelry findings, crepe paper, ephemera, and images.

Instructions for the *Wizard of Oz* Peat-Pot Pocket Posy

1. Paint a harlequin pattern on the outside of the peat pot.

2. Attach a vintage *Wizard of Oz* image to the peat pot with Modge Podge. See image selections, page 115. Apply a border of Elmer's Gel Glue around the image, and then sprinkle with red glitter; shake off any excess.

3. Punch two holes in opposite sides of the peat-pot upper edge. Thread the ends of the 12" (30.5 cm) craft wire through the holes, leaving 1" (2.5 cm) of wire at each end. Wrap the extra 1" (2.5 cm) of wire back around itself to secure.

4. Wrap designer ribbon around the wire handle and tie a fanciful knot at each end. Cut a triangle into the ribbon ends, and then add a line of glue to the cut edges to prevent fraying.

5. Pinch off small pieces of the Model Magic and roll into tiny balls. Attach the balls to the harlequin points on the peat pot with Elmer's Gel Glue. Paint the balls with gold metallic paint.

6. Finish the pot with rhinestones and vintage trim.

✴ ✴ ✴

HELPFUL TIPS AND ALTERNATIVES

✱ Substitute vintage sheet music for the *Wizard of Oz* image.

✱ Use hot-glue to attach crepe paper and a sequin-trim border around the pot upper edge.

✱ Finish the pot with a paper medallion, ribbon, rhinestones, and more glitter.

✱ Use tinsel chenille stems for a handle instead of wire.

✱ Turn carnival or raffle tickets into tiny banners or wands. Glue the tickets to a toothpick or piece of wire and add glitter.

VINTAGE-STYLE PAPER DOLLS

WHETHER WE ARE EIGHT YEARS OLD OR EIGHTY, THERE IS ALWAYS A SPECIAL PLACE IN OUR HEARTS FOR DOLLS.

I still have all my favorite dolls from when I was a child. This paper-doll project is the first in a series that will teach you how to make your own fanciful dolls.

Instructions for the Marie Antoinette paper doll

Materials

- ★ basic tool kit; see page 13
- ★ decorative paper (designer, handmade, wallpaper, tissue, crepe paper, etc)
- ★ 2" x 5" (5.1 x 12.7 cm) rectangle of poster board
- ★ ribbons, trims, lace
- ★ rescued jewelry: rhinestone button or pin, broken necklace, pendant
- ★ rhinestones, beads
- ★ vintage images, ephemera
- ★ glitter and glitter-paint pens
- ★ white puff paint
- ★ cotton balls
- ★ glue: Modge Podge, basic white glue

1. Make a copy of the Marie Antoinette image on page 116. Also make a reversed copy of the image. Adhere one image onto a piece of poster board with a foam brush dipped in Modge Podge; let dry. Recut out the image. Then glue the remaining image to the back. (If your software doesn't have a mirror-image feature, cover the back with designer paper.)

2. Add a cotton ball for hair. Partially pull apart a white cotton ball, and use white glue to adhere it to the hair portion of the image. When dry, cover the cotton hair with white puff paint, smear the paint gently with your finger, sprinkle with white glitter, and add a rhinestone. The puff paint will hold the glitter and rhinestone in place.

3. Add extra embellishments and glitter as desired. Use dots of puff paint to create imitation pearls.

Helpful Tips and Alternatives

- ✶ For a sugary look, use white puff paint for the hair and sprinkle it with light-pink glitter while the paint is still wet.

- ✶ Turn your paper doll into a cupcake queen by cutting out a cupcake image and gluing it to your doll's head to look like a cupcake crown.

THE PRINCESS AND THE PEA PAPER DOLL ASSEMBLAGE

The Princess and the Pea HAS BEEN A FAVORITE STORY OF MINE IN ALL ITS VARIOUS FORMS. SO I WAS INSPIRED TO CREATE MY OWN VERSION, WHICH ADDS A NURSERY-RHYME ASPECT.

This project combines an advanced-style paper doll with dimensional props made from paper, fabric, and wood.

MATERIALS

- ★ basic tool kit; see page 13
- ★ decorative paper (designer, handmade, wallpaper, tissue, crepe paper, etc)
- ★ fabric remnants
- ★ ribbons, trims, lace
- ★ vintage images, ephemera
- ★ four 12" (30.5 cm) -lengths of craft wire
- ★ Model Magic modeling material
- ★ 3" x 5" (7.6 x 12.7 cm) wooden doll bed
- ★ 5" (12.7 cm) -tall wooden dollhouse door
- ★ 3" x 5" (7.6 x 12.7 cm) rectangle of poster board
- ★ glitter and glitter-paint pens
- ★ acrylic paint (black, brown, light blue, light green, pink, cream, gold)
- ★ crackle medium
- ★ glue: Modge Podge, Elmer's Gel Glue, industrial glue, hot-glue

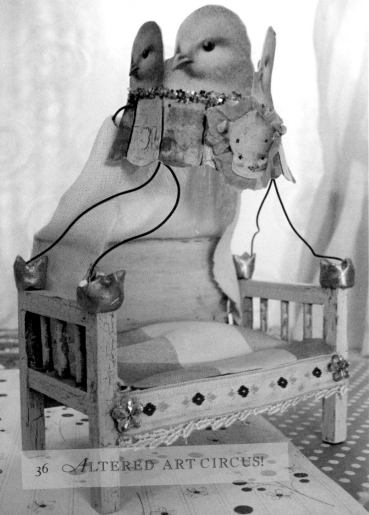

Altered Art Circus!

INSTRUCTIONS FOR THE BED

1. Glue a wooden doll-closet door to one long side of a wooden doll bed with industrial glue; let dry.

2. Paint the doll-bed assemblage with pink paint; let dry. Then add crackle medium; let dry. Mix light blue and light-green paint together for the final paint layer. (See page 16 for more on crackling and aging techniques.)

3. Wrap a strand of wire around the top of each bedpost. Wrap the wire around the post three times for durability.

4. To make the bed crown, color photocopy four chick images, (See page 115) and glue the chicks side by side on a strip of poster board with Modge Podge. When dry, cut around the chick's heads, and then measure 1" (2.5 cm) from the base of the chicks. Cut the lower edge in a scallop pattern. Referring to the image, paint each scallop section with a different acrylic paint in the colors of your choice.

5. Glue a whimsical pig image (see page 115) to aqua crepe paper, and then add the image to the scallop portion of the bed crown. Apply a line of Elmer's Gel Glue between the chicks and scalloped edge, and sprinkle with pink-glitter flakes.

6. Punch a hole on each end of the bed crown. Twist the ends of the two wire lengths on the left side of the bed together, and then thread them into the left crown hole. Repeat with wires on the right side. Join two wires together, twisting them into a circular shape behind the crown.

7. Cut a fabric rectangle about 4" x 6" (10.2 x 15.2 cm). Hot-glue one edge to the bed-crown wire, and drape the opposite edge around the back of the bed.

8. Mold four small crowns from Model Magic, and then shape them around the bedposts to hide the wire wrapping; let dry. Paint the bedpost crowns gold.

9. Hot-glue pink fabric to the bed surface as a bedspread. Add lace and ribbon to the remaining long side of the bed. Finish each end of the ribbon and trim with a flower rhinestone.

INSTRUCTIONS FOR THE PRINCESS PAPER DOLL

1. Cut out a paper doll image of choice and glue it to the poster board with a foam brush dipped in Modge Podge. Let dry, and then recut out the image.

2. Add a skirt made from two fabrics. Place the fabrics right side up, one on top of the other, with the bottom layer a little longer to look like a petticoat. Working with both layers as one, bunch the upper edge to gather it, and hot-glue the edge around the paper doll's waist. Tie a thin wire ribbon around the skirt and add a flower rhinestone.

3. For the princess hat, roll suede paper into a cone shape and hot-glue closed; let dry. Hot-glue the cone to the doll's head. Embellish with a rhinestone garland, crepe paper, and more glitter.

4. For the wand, reduce a copy of the pig image, hot-glue it to a rusty wire, and then sprinkle with glitter.

★ ★ ★

HELPFUL TIPS AND ALTERNATIVES

✶ Make a pillow using two same-size squares cut from a paper bag. Hot-glue three edges together, stuff with a little batting, and then hot-glue the opening closed. Paint the pillow with your favorite colors.

✶ Make several small pillows and stack them on the doll bed for a different look.

✶ Age and stiffen the lace with liquid starch mixed with a dab of brown acrylic paint.

Throughout history, pointed hats have been important
accessories in a variety of cultures. Some historians suggest that
the pointed hat is actually a witch's hat dating back to the ancient
Etruscans, whose coins from the city of Luna depict a person on one
side wearing a pointed hat. Many believe this to be the goddess Diana, who
is primarily associated with witches. Further study suggests that witch hats are
related to dunce hats, popular in royal courts during the fifteenth century. These
hats are also similar to hats worn by the Welsh during the same period. The Welsh hats
were for warmth and protection and to scare birds away from stealing their crops.

While researching the topic of hats, I stumbled across images of Marie Antoinette and was
instantly inspired by her style. I always loved the chalky-white wigs and pastel ball gowns worn
during her time period. I wanted to merge these elements together to create this opera-hat doll
I call "Marie Antoinette Soirée," which can also be used as a centerpiece.

INSTRUCTIONS FOR MARIE ANTOINETTE SOIREE:

MATERIALS

* basic tool kit; see page 13
* paper (designer, handmade, wallpaper, tissue paper, etc)
* poster board or cardstock (large sheet, any color)
* fabric remnants
* ribbons, trims, lace
* jewelry findings, holiday ornaments
* vintage images, ephemera
* glitter and glitter-paint pens
* acrylic paint (black, brown, light blue, light green, pink, cream, 14-karat gold)
* gesso
* gel medium
* glue: Modge Podge, tacky glue, hot-glue
* other: rhinestones, metal pieces, letters from foam, wood, or chipboard

1. Measure your head to determine the size of your hat or centerpiece.

2. Enlarge the cone pattern (located on page 116) about 200 percent on a copy machine or on a personal scanner, and then print the image.

3. Trace the enlarged cone pattern onto a sheet of designer paper. Cut out the shape, and glue it to the poster board with Modge Podge. Use a rolling pin to roll out any air bubbles and paper creases. Trim the poster board to match the designer paper.

4. Roll into a cone shape, and apply a line of hot-glue at the one end to secure. Apply pressure to help seal the join.

5. Enlarge and cut out the image of Marie Antoinette to be about 8" (20.3 cm) tall from the waist up. (See page 116.) Glue the image onto poster board with Modge Podge. When dry, trim the poster board even with the image, and then attach her to the cone point with hot-glue.

6. Measure from the cone tip to the lower edge, and then cut a fabric rectangle the determined measure by about 24" (61 cm). Hot-glue the two 24" (61 cm) edges around the cone—gather and glue one edge at Marie's waist, and the other to the cone's lower edge. Form the skirt front by hot-gluing another piece of fabric to the cone. (See the image at right.)

7. To make the side bustles, pinch the fabric and slip stitch the pinch in place. Or, if you wish, use hot-glue to hold the fabric in place.

8. Hot-glue vintage fringe to the cone lower edge. Add vintage trim to the skirt sides and a gold satin bow to the skirt upper back. Add a rhinestone button, fabric flowers, and more glitter to complete the embellishments.

9. For ties, hot-glue two ribbons on each side of the hat along the lower inside edge.

★ ★ ★

HELPFUL TIPS AND ALTERNATIVES

✦ In place of a vintage image, use the bust of a porcelain doll or tassel doll for the top of the hat; glue in place with industrial glue.

✦ If the glued images crimp or get bubbles, try heat setting them. To do this use an iron set on low heat with no steam, place the glued paper base on the ironing board, cover with a piece of muslin fabric, and iron until flat.

FAIRYTALE PAGEANT CROWN

THE ART OF CREATING FANTASY ADORNMENTS
HAS STARTED TO SOAR, PARTIALLY DUE TO THE CRAZE
OF WIZARD AND FAIRY FILMS. FROM MOVIES TO DOLLS,
EVERYONE WANTS TO BE A PART OF THE FANTASY WORLD.

In this project you will complete an enchanting fantasy crown constructed with a variety of techniques and filled with elements that reflect your royal muse. Now you will be queen for a day!

Instructions for the Pixie-Pageant Crown

Materials

- ★ basic tool kit; see page 13
- ★ paper (designer, handmade, wallpaper, tissue, and crepe paper, etc)
- ★ poster board or cardstock (large sheet, any color)
- ★ ribbons, trims, lace
- ★ jewelry findings, holiday ornaments
- ★ vintage images, ephemera
- ★ Model Magic modeling material
- ★ chipboard letters
- ★ glitter and glitter-paint pens
- ★ acrylic paint (black, brown, light blue, light green, pink, cream, 14-karat gold)
- ★ gesso
- ★ crackle medium
- ★ glue: Modge Podge, tacky glue, hot glue

1. Measure your head to determine the size of your crown.

2. Make your own pattern or enlarge the pixie-pageant-crown template (on page 117) on a copy machine; cut out.

3. Trace the pattern onto the poster board; cut out.

4. Apply paper or fabric to both sides of the poster-board crown with glue, rolling out the air bubbles with a rolling pin; let dry.

5. Create a harlequin pattern on the crown by drawing connecting X-shapes with a pencil. Paint the resulting diamond shapes black; let dry. Apply crackle medium; let dry until tacky. Finish with white and light blue paint, alternating the colors in the diamonds; let dry.

6. Reinforce the pixie image by gluing it onto poster board with Modge Podge. Recut out the image and attach it to the crown with tacky glue.

7. Roll a piece of the Model Magic into a ball, and then continue to roll and flatten it into a long rope with a ¼" (6 mm) diameter.

8. Glue the Model Magic rope to the crown upper borders by applying tacky glue to the border and gently patting the Model Magic rope in place. Let the Model Magic dry for 24 hours.

9. For the green finials on the crown I used five small Christmas ornaments. Thread a wire through the hole of each ornament; wrap the wire around itself to secure. Punch two holes in the crown on each side of the image. Thread the other end of the ornament wire through each of the holes and wrap to close. Add the remaining ornament to the center of the crown's upper edge. Instead of punching a hole, glue the wire to the back of the crown with industrial glue, and then cover it with the same paper as the crown.

10. Add a designer ribbon to the crown's lower edge with tacky glue.

11. Arrange small chipboard letters to spell "Pixie," and attach them to the crown with tacky glue. When the letters are secured, lightly spread more glue over them, and sprinkle with pink and red glitter.

12. To close the crown and keep it on your head, glue a ribbon to each end. Tie the ribbon closed with a bow similar to how you would tie an apron.

✫ ✫ ✫
HELPFUL TIPS
AND ALTERNATIVES

✫ Create paper medallions from vintage images cut into circles. Reinforce the images by gluing them onto poster board and then backing the image with crepe paper; add glitter.

✫ Paint a dollar-store plastic crown with wood glue; let dry. Then paint the crown with aqua, light green, and copper for a patina metal look. To do this, pick up a little of each paint on the brush, and then paint so the colors blend on the crown and create a mottled effect. Decorate as desired.

The Traveling Bumbelinas

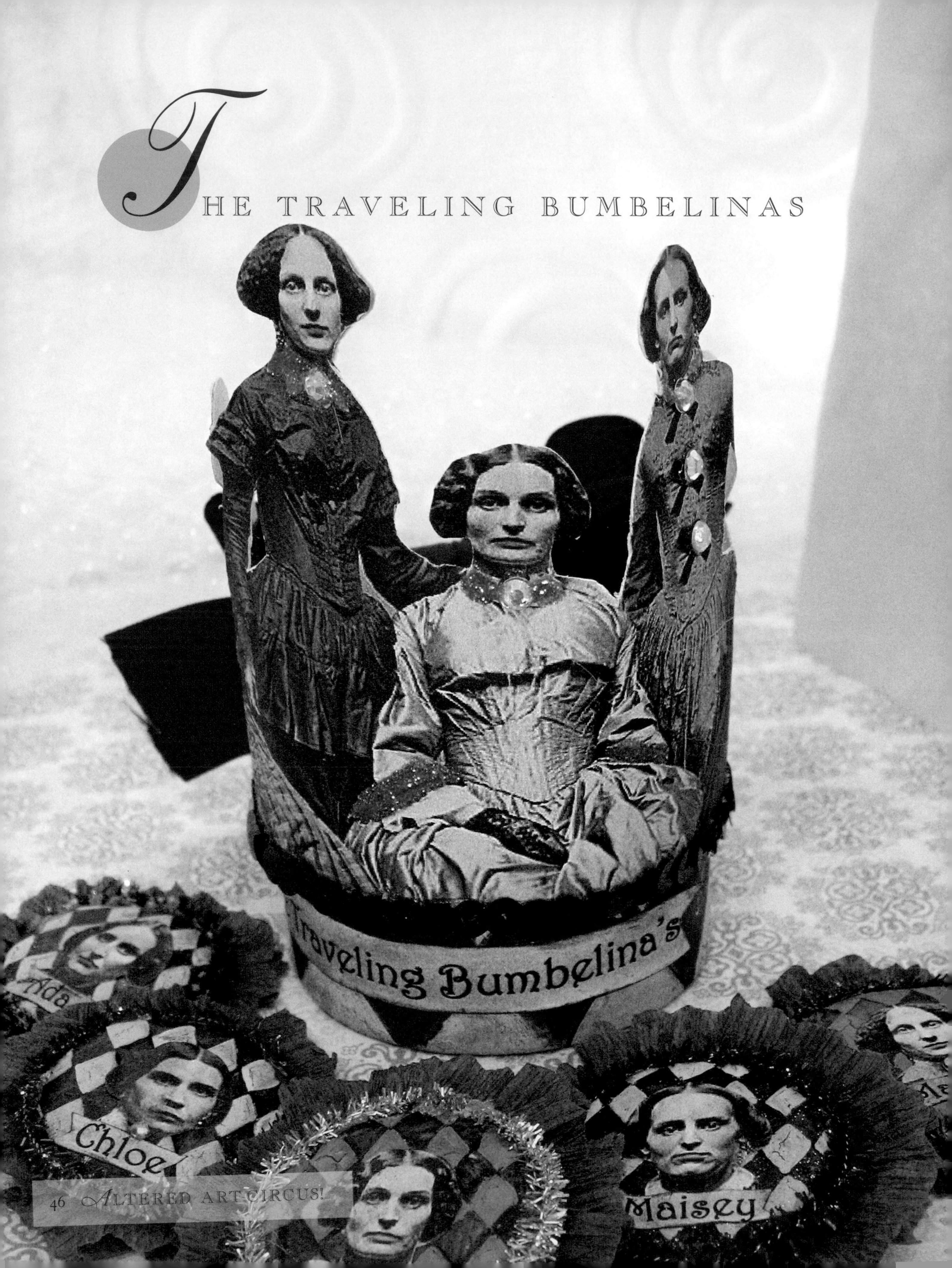
Traveling Bumbelina's
Ada
Chloe
Maisey

The Traveling Bumbelinas
are five sisters
who grew up around the carnival.
Their father,
A. G. Bumbelina, created
the Bumbelina Traveling Circus,
which has journeyed all over the world.

Today the Bumbelina sisters—Ada,
Chloe, Maisey, Maude, and Winnie—carry
on their father's tradition and travel around the
world, only this time they do it in the summer and
host an end-of-the-season masquerade ball.

Bumbelina Tokens are awarded after winning each game
so you may collect your prize at the toy booth.
Come with me and enter the world of
The Traveling Bumbelinas.

MATERIALS

★ basic tool kit; see page 13

★ small round papier-mâche box

★ plastic poker chips

★ paper (designer, handmade, wallpaper, tissue, and crepe paper, etc)

★ ribbon, sequin trim

★ tinsel chenille stems

★ vintage images, ephemera

★ Model Magic modeling material

★ harlequin rubber stamp

★ glitter and glitter-paint pens

★ acrylic paint (black, brown, light blue, light green, pink, cream, 14-karat gold)

★ crackle medium

★ glue: Modge Podge, tacky glue, hot glue

INSTRUCTIONS FOR THE TRAVELING BUMBELINA CROWN BOX

1. Paint the papier-mâche box with black acrylic paint; let dry. Repaint the box with crackle medium; let dry until tacky. Then draw a simple harlequin pattern on the box with connecting X-shapes.

Paint the resulting diamond shapes with red acrylic paint and the spaces with pink paint. (Refer to basic techniques on page 16 for crackling techniques.)

2. Glue the image onto poster board with Modge Podge, and then recut the image. See pages 116 and 118 for image choices. Attach the lower edge of the image to the rim of the box lid with tacky glue so the image stands upright.

3. Use tacky glue to attach a strand of black sequin trim to the image lower edge.

4. Add a banner with "The Traveling Bumbelinas" typed on it. Use the computer to type the banner, print it out, and then glue the banner to the box.

5. Apply glue lightly to parts of the images, sprinkle with pink glitter, and add tiny rhinestones.

Instructions for the Traveling Bumbelina Tokens

1. Apply glue to one side of a plastic poker chip and cover with Model Magic. Press a harlequin stamp (large enough to cover the poker chip) into the Model Magic; remove. When the Model Magic dries, add color to the small diamond shapes with acrylic paint.

2. Cut out the heads of the Bumbelina sisters and glue each to a poker chip with tacky glue. Print out their names on the computer, use shoe polish to age the names (refer to the basic techniques on page 16), and glue the names to the poker chips with tacky glue.

3. Wrap a tinsel chenille strip around the poker-chip edges and adhere with hot glue. Add crepe-paper fringe by gathering and gluing a strip of crepe paper to the back of the poker chip at the edges. Finish the back of the token with a designer-paper circle.

4. Add tiny rhinestones to some of the tokens.

✦✦✦

Helpful Tips and Alternatives

✫ Make tokens using individual photos of your family or favorite storybook characters.

✫ Trade these tokens with other artists, just as you would artist trading cards.

CARNIVAL THEATRES

THE TRAVELING-CIRCUS OPERA WAS CREATED 100 YEARS AGO BY THE FAMOUS OPERA SINGER PIERRE LE ROUGE TO SHOWCASE CREATURES GREAT AND SMALL, EXPRESSING THEIR TALENTS TO THE REST OF THE WORLD AND SHINING IN THE SPOTLIGHT FOREVER.

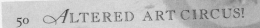

Today Pierre's great grandchildren continue the tradition with unusual shows such as: Miss Zara, The Lioness of Magic; Sierra, The Sea Fairy of Cape May; Thumbelina, The Tiniest Woman on Earth; and The Fiji Mermaid of Madagascar. Two must-sees are the Tent of Crypto Zoology and the Ballerina Giraffes.

MATERIALS

★ 5½" (14 cm) -tall dollhouse wardrobe cabinet (found in the wood section of the craft store)

★ package of wooden wheels with ³⁄₁₆" (4.8 mm) holes, set of four

★ package of ³⁄₁₆" (4.8 mm) -diameter wooden dowels

★ package of small wooden blocks

★ bag of tiny seashells

★ wooden beads with holes to accommodate the dowels

★ paper (designer, handmade, wallpaper, tissue, and crepe paper, etc)

★ ribbon, sequin trim

★ tinsel chenille stems

★ vintage images, ephemera

★ small candy tart wrapper in red

★ glitter and glitter-paint pens

★ acrylic paint (black, brown, purple, electric blue, light blue, light green, pink, red, yellow, white, cream, 14-karat gold)

★ Model Magic modeling material

★ glue: Modge Podge, tacky glue, hot glue

★ other: rhinestones, beads, wire, doll hats, top hats

INSTRUCTIONS FOR THE TRAVELING-CIRCUS OPERA BOX

1. Remove the doors from the doll closet with pliers. Simply twist and tug at the doors, they will pop right off because the wood is so soft. The box will be in its upright position when the project is complete.

2. Paint the box exterior with red paint. Paint the box interior pink and the front borders light green.

3. Measure the inside of the box, and cut designer paper to fit. Use one paper for the sides and a different paper for the back. Glue the papers in place with Modge Podge. Insert a vintage circus image on the back wall of the closet over the decorative paper.

4. Cut out the Thumbelina image (see pages 119 and 120). Reinforce the image by gluing it to poster board with a foam brush dipped in Modge Podge; let dry. Trim the poster board even with the image, and then hot-glue the image's feet and ankles to a small wooden block. Hot-glue the block to the lower right-front of the closet opening. (See the image at left.)

5. Make the curtain banner. Cut a 1½" x 6" (3.8 x 15.2 cm) strip of heavy paper. Use decorative scissors with scalloped blades to cut one long edge of the paper. Paint the banner pink, and sprinkle with red glitter. Hot-glue the strip to the upper right and left front edges of the box.

6. Embellish the top of the box with a handmade cupcake ornament. To make the cupcake ornament, roll out a long rope of Model Magic that is about ½" (1.3 cm) in diameter. Coil the rope inside the candy tart wrapper to form cupcake icing, repeat as necessary to fill the wrapper. Finish the cupcake with pink paint and glitter. Hot-glue the cupcake ornament in place.

7. Cut a pink tinsel chenille strip in half, forming two strips. Hot-glue a strip to each side of the cart front, and then hot-glue five red oval rhinestones in a flower shape at the top of each tinsel strip. Add a pearl to the flower center and sprinkle with glitter.

8. Embellish the box with small banners with "Thumbelina" written on them, more images, and lettering.

9. To attach the wheels, cut two wooden dowels that extend ¾" (1.9 cm) from each side of the cart base. The extra length will be inserted into the wheels. Glue the dowels in place on the cart underside. Paint the wheel rims with pink paint and the wheel face with light green paint; let dry. Slip a wheel onto each dowel end. Then glue a small wooden bead onto the end of each dowel, leaving a tiny space (as thin as paper) between the bead and the wheel. This will secure the wheel on the dowel and allow it to roll. Finish the wheels with glitter.

✳ ✳ ✳

HELPFUL TIPS
AND ALTERNATIVES

To make other circus boxes, follow the directions for the Thumbelina box except:

✷ Use a variety of seashore, carnival, and fairy images.

✷ Glue tiny shells around the box.

✷ Use a silver tinsel chenille strip to make a small crown for the figure. Bend one end to equal the width of the figure's head, and then bend the remainder of the strip to form points of the crown. Trim any excess chenille strip and twist the wire ends closed. Hot glue the finished crown to her head.

✷ Attach tiny doll embellishments, such as hats, frames, and marble beads.

✷ For wands, cut a thin piece of wire, use pliers to bend it into a squiggly circle at one end, glue a tiny shape to the squiggly circle, and then hot-glue the wand in place.

✷ If you are unable to locate an unfinished doll closet or cabinet, try using a similar small shadow box, a papier-mâché box, or wooden box.

✷ If you can't find wooden beads, use pony beads to secure the wheels. Or shape small balls from Model Magic and glue them over the dowel ends; paint and embellish with glitter.

✷ Create a circus by using your family photos in place of Lady LeRouge, Sierra, or Thumbelina. Create a character personality for each family member. For example, my mom loves tea— I could say, "Now presenting, Joan the Tea Lady."

✷ Remember when working with hot glue, pins, X-acto knives, or chemicals to proceed with caution and always read the manufacturer's labels.

CHAPTER THREE

Captured-Jar Fairies, Specimens, and Wands

★★★

Remembering my first day in seventh-grade science class,

I was mesmerized by all the specimens in glass jars sitting on wooden shelves. The jars were filled with crystals, butterflies, and weird specimens immersed in colored liquids.

★★★

As I began to explore the essence of nature, science, and unsolved mysteries, such as

The Cottingley Fairies and Loch Ness Monster, my curiosity rose, and led to an awakening of my imagination.

★★★

Recapturing these moments in time was something I had to do.

Glass domes, balls, and jars all symbolize tiny worlds to me. Like Alice peering through the looking glass, I aimed to look into another world filled with magic. In this chapter you will see tiny worlds through my glasses, small portals into another place. I call these portals captured jars and specimens.

{ *No tiny creatures were hurt in the making of these pieces.* }

Captured Cupcake-Princess Wands and Wand Jar

I HAVE BEEN CREATING IN A NEW COLOR PALETTE, WHICH I REFER TO AS CUPCAKE CHIC — A CREAMY BLEND OF COLORS ASSOCIATED WITH THE 1940S AND '50S.

For this project I wanted to create a piece reminiscent of that era, and mixed in the feel of apothecary and glam; all completed through a glass bottle, paints, images, and lots of glitz.

MATERIALS

- ★ basic tool kit; see page 13

- ★ small- to medium-size glass jars with lids, apothecary bottles

- ★ package of small wooden square blocks

- ★ package of ⅛" (3 mm) bamboo skewers or wooden dowels

- ★ bag of reindeer moss (found in most craft and home decorating stores)

- ★ bag of cotton balls

- ★ paper (designer, handmade, wallpaper, tissue, crepe paper, etc)

- ★ fabric scraps

- ★ ribbon, sequin trim

- ★ black embroidery floss

- ★ tinsel chenille stems

- ★ vintage images, ephemera

- ★ Model Magic modeling material

- ★ glitter and glitter-paint pens

- ★ puffy-paint pens (white, black, and pink)

- ★ acrylic paint (black, brown, purple, electric blue, light blue, light green, pink, red, yellow, white, cream, 14-karat gold)

- ★ glue: Modge Podge, tacky glue, hot glue

- ★ tools: paper heat tool

- ★ clear sandwich bag

- ★ other: rhinestones, beads, wire, raffia-paper ribbon

INSTRUCTIONS FOR THE CAPTURED CUPCAKE-PRINCESS WANDS

1. Paint three bamboo skewers with black acrylic paint; let dry. Paint crackle medium over the skewer; let dry until tacky. Then paint each skewer with a different color—pink, blue, or purple; let dry. (Refer to page 16 for crackling and aging techniques).

2. Glue an image onto poster board with Modge Podge. Choose three vintage images. See page 119 for one image selection. Then recut the images out and hot glue them to the painted skewers.

3. Create tiny cupcake hats by rolling two small balls of Model Magic, glue one on top of the other, and pinch the top. Cut a narrow paper strip and glue it around the lower ball to form a cupcake wrapper. Paint and embellish the upper ball for the cupcake icing, and then insert the image head partially into the cupcake from the underside; let dry.

4. Create wings for each fairy with a tinsel chenille strip. Bend the chenille-strip ends in a oval toward the center, and then hot-glue the center to the back of the image.

5. Embellish the wands with rhinestones and ribbon.

Instructions for the Wand Jar

1. Paint the outside of an apothecary jar with black acrylic paint; let dry. Then paint crackle medium over the jar; let dry until tacky. Mix light green and light-blue paint over the crackle medium. (Refer to basic techniques section on page 16 for crackling and aging techniques.)

2. Wrap a piece of black grosgrain ribbon around the neck of the jar, knot in place, and tie a bow.

3. Make a small cupcake lid for the jar. Press a ball of Model Magic partially into the jar opening, and then pull it back out. Wrap the portion that will protrude from the jar with a strip of paper to form the cupcake wrapper. For the icing, make two smaller balls of Model Magic and glue them to the larger ball. Paint the top of the cupcake, and then decorate the cupcake and wrapper. When dry, the lid will fit nicely in the jar opening (when the jar is not holding the wands).

4. Embellish the jar with a rhinestone pin, glitter, letters, and more trimmings.

Instructions for the Captured Cupcake Princess

1. Find your cupcake-princess image and cut out. Glue the image to poster board with Modge Podge; let dry. Trim the poster board even with the image, and then glue the lower edge to the front of the small wooden block; let dry.

2. Glue the base of the small wooden block to the interior base of the glass jar; let dry.

3. In a clear sandwich bag add two tablespoons of pink paint and four cotton balls. Mix the pink paint into the cotton balls by squeezing and kneading the bag until the cotton balls are coated, about five minutes.

4. Remove the colored cotton balls, place on a piece of poster board, and let dry for a few hours.

5. Apply a generous amount of tacky glue to the inside bottom of the glass jar. Place the colored cotton balls inside the jar, making sure to cover up the wooden block.

6. Cut out a background image to fit inside the jar. Position the image behind the cupcake princess image.

7. Measure the jar height. Cut two fabric strips the determined length for the curtain panels. Slightly pleat each panel, and use tacky glue to secure the panels inside the jar on the left and right of the princess; let dry.

8. Make a cupcake lid for the jar. Roll a ball of Model Magic with a diameter slightly smaller than the jar lid; glue the ball to the lid. Roll out two long Model Magic ropes about ½" (1.3 cm) in diameter. Coil the ropes on top of the ball to form cupcake icing; repeat as necessary. Paint the cupcake pink and add glitter. If desired add a cherry made from a small ball of Model Magic painted red. Finish the cupcake by cutting a 2" (5.1 cm) -wide strip of paper and gluing it to the lid rim to form the cupcake wrapper. Embellish the wrapper with lettering and glitter. Glue the lid in place.

SPECIMEN COZY AND THE FIJI MERMAID JAR FAIRY

COZIES AREN'T JUST FOR TEAPOTS ANYMORE. NO CAPTURED-JAR FAIRY WOULD BE COMPLETE WITHOUT A COZY OF THEIR OWN TO PROVIDE THEM WITH WARMTH, PRIVACY, AND PROTECTION FROM THE BRIGHT SUNSHINE.

This project will show you how to make a custom cozy made from
fabric, ribbons, images, and more for each jar fairy in your collection.

Instructions for the Specimen Cozy

Materials

★ basic tool kit; see page 13

★ ½ yard (45.7 cm) of printed fabric

★ crepe paper

★ ribbon

★ pom-pom fringe

★ enlarged photocopy of your jar fairy

★ glitter and glitter-paint pens

★ glue: basic white glue, hot glue

★ other: charms, chipboard letters, rhinestones, pearls, tags

1. Begin by cutting a 12" x 20" (30.5 x 50.8 cm) rectangle of fabric. Fold 1" (2.5 cm) of fabric to the wrong side around the edges; hot-glue the fabric in place.

2. Fold the fabric in half with wrong sides facing and the edges aligned. The folded fabric should measure 10" x 12" (25.4 x 30.5 cm). Cut four 10 ½" (26.7 cm) lengths of ribbon. Insert the ends of two ribbons between the fabric layers on each of the two shorter fabric edges. Place the ribbons 2" (5.1 cm) on either side of the edge centers; hot-glue in place. Position the header of pom-pom fringe between the fabric layers on the long edge opposite the fold; hot-glue the fringe in place.

3. Hot-glue the cozy side seams and lower edge closed. (See the example above.)

4. Cut out your enlarged image, glue it to the cozy with white glue, embellish with crepe paper, charms, glitter, and a description tag or story.

★ ★ ★

Helpful Tips and Alternatives

✫ Use decorative paper in place of the fabric.

✫ Cut a decorative wine-bottle bag in half and embellish.

Instructions for the Fiji Mermaid Jar Fairy

1. Select and copy an image for your Fiji Mermaid. Cut out the image, and then glue it to poster board with Modge Podge; let dry. Trim the poster board around the image, and glue the image's feet to the front of the wooden block; let dry.

2. Glue the base of the wooden block to the inside base of the glass jar; let dry.

3. Apply a generous amount of tacky glue to the inside bottom of the glass jar and remaining sides of the wooden block. Cover the glue with reindeer moss, making sure to cover the wooden block.

4. Cut out the background image to fit, and place it inside the jar.

5. Cut out three small lantern images. To hang the lanterns, sandwich black embroidery floss between the images and small pieces of paper that are glued together. Glue the end of the embroidery floss to the lid underside with tacky glue, making sure the lanterns hang inside the jar.

6. Glue the lid in place with tacky glue.

7. Paint the lid with blue acrylic paint, embellish with two different faces of the Fiji mermaid, lettering, and glitter. Tie raffia ribbon around neck of the jar.

8. Print the legend of the Fiji mermaid onto parchment paper. Use a paper heat tool to lightly burn the edges. Also stain the edges with walnut ink to finish, and then glue the legend to the back of the jar with tacky glue.

CRYSTAL-BALL WANDS

EVER SINCE I WAS A CHILD I HAVE BEEN OBSESSED WITH FAIRIES AND WANDS, ALWAYS TRYING TO CREATE A UNIQUE AND SPECIAL ONE.

As an adult I found myself doing the same thing. Then about a year ago I saw a glowing and sparkling light swerve around me at a fairy festival. This prompted me to re-create that moment with a crystal ball wand, which contains a fairy, glitter, and lots of enchantment.

Instructions for the Crystal-Ball Wand

1. Reduce a vintage fairy image so it is large enough to see and will fit in the glass ornament. Decorate your fairy with wings and a three-dimensional cone-shaped paper hat. Paint the hat and embellish with clear glitter.

2. Insert the fairy into the ornament by gently rolling and slipping it inside. Glue the fairy's feet to the ornament rim with a dab of hot glue.

3. Coat the ornament rim with white glue and stuff Model Magic into the opening. Dip the end of the wooden dowel into white glue and insert it into the Model Magic. Balance the wand on a flat surface with the wooden end slightly elevated, and let cure overnight.

4. Paint the wooden dowel with light green paint and let dry.

5. Embellish the wand with accents made from Model Magic, a paper crown, charms, crystal beads, velvet ribbons, and glitter.

★ ★ ★

Helpful Tips and Alternatives

✻ Glue a small piece of reindeer moss inside the base of the ornament before you insert the Model Magic.

✻ Substitute clear caulk in place of the Model Magic.

Materials

★ basic tool kit; see page 13

★ small- to medium-size glass-ornament bulb

★ ½" (1.3 cm) -diameter wooden dowel

★ paper (designer, handmade, wallpaper, tissue, crepe paper, etc)

★ ribbon, sequin trim

★ tinsel chenille stems

★ vintage images, ephemera

★ Model Magic modeling material

★ glitter and glitter-paint pens

★ puffy-paint pens (white, black, pink)

★ acrylic paint (black, light green, white)

★ glue: basic white glue, hot glue

★ other: rhinestones, crystal beads, charms, ribbon

CHAPTER FOUR

Art Cards, Pockets, and Spellbinding Books

★ ★ ★

Artist trading cards are miniature works of art, which can be traded or sold. These tiny masterpieces actually began centuries ago as painted wallet-size portraits and became quite the rage during the sixteenth century.

The development of photography eventually replaced the realistic portraits. Photography had the ability to capture a moment in life, to freeze a memory, and allow it to become a part of our past. The viewer was able to revisit a favorite holiday or vacation, and to gaze into the eyes of a loved one when they were absent. The Victorians played with this development by mixing photos with the unusual and fantasy to create postcards, which are still collected today.

During the 1800s, artists traded art cards of their work with other artists as a source of information and inspiration, which we still do today. Trading art cards became popular again during 1997, in Zurich, Switzerland, due to M. Vanci Stirnemann. This trend has since spread all over the world. Artists from everywhere are creating these inexpensive miniatures for trade and self-promotion, all staying within the standard dimensions of 2½" x 3½" (6.4 x 8.9 cm), the same size as a baseball or playing card.

Besides having a standard dimension, artist trading cards have a set of rules, depending on the group trading them. Some artists believe since the original idea is to trade these works that artist trading cards should not to be sold for profit. Others disagree and create works, or limited-edition prints of their art, which are sold. Artists sign and date the back of their art cards, which also includes the title, series, piece number, and their contact information.

Artist trading cards are created on a base of poster board, chipboard, matte board, cardstock, Italian watercolor paper, canvas paper, a playing card, balsa wood, fabric, or metal. They are created with a variety of found materials and in a multitude of art mediums. I make, trade, and sell my creations. The art cards I create have a variety of themes based on children's stories, fairytales, and history. I make flat art cards, three-dimensional cards, paper-doll cards, card pockets, card books, and art-card prints of my digital art. In the next few pages you will learn how to make your own art-card pockets, books, and single art-card whimsies. Look for inspiration in your surroundings, and start creating your own artist trading cards.

CIRCUSOLOGY ART-CARD POCKETBOOK

For this Circusology project, the worlds of art, circuses, sideshows, carnivals, mysteries, daring, intrigue, and fantasy meld to become an epitome of this book.

I have coined the term *Circusology*, to signify the study and the history of the circus arts. This project is a glimpse into the art circus, which is filled with sideshow and circus memorabilia. You will create this circusology art card on chipboard, and then layer it with a paper accordion book, lots of images, and embellishments.

INSTRUCTIONS FOR THE CIRCUSOLOGY ART-CARD POCKETBOOK

MATERIALS

★ basic tool kit; see page 13

★ paper (designer, handmade, wallpaper, tissue, and crepe paper, etc)

★ poster board

★ matte board

★ ribbons, trims, lace, etc.

★ jewelry findings

★ vintage images, ephemera

★ wire

★ glitter and glitter-paint pens

★ glue: Modge Podge, Elmer's Gel Glue, tacky glue, hot glue

★ other: rhinestones, beads

1. Cut two 2½" x 3½" (6.4 x 8.9 cm) rectangles from the chipboard.

2. Cut a 3½" x 15" (8.9 x 38.1 cm) rectangle of poster board. Measure 2½" from one short end and mark a line across the poster board. Draw four more lines spacing them 2½" apart to create six standard size art-trading-card spaces—these measurements should be precise.

3. Accordion-fold the poster board strip on the marked lines. Glue the end sections of the folded poster board to the two chipboard rectangles with tacky glue; let dry.

4. For the front and back covers, choose a mix of papers and images for the backgrounds. I attached designer sea-green paper to the front cover with gel glue. Create a big-top circus tent with a 2" x 5½" (5.1 x 14 cm) strip of poster board covered with a tent-top image. To form the tent top, arch the cut paper strip over the upper portion of the front cover. Fold under the strip ends ½" (1.3 cm) and use tacky glue to attach the folded ends to the front-cover edges. Embellish the tent top with crepe-paper fringe, sequins, beads, glitter, and lettering. Decorate the back cover with a yard of ribbon glued to the surface with tacky glue; let dry.

5. Begin decorating the pages of the accordion-fold book. The three-dimensional and removable images were reinforced with poster board. See page 119 for image selections. Glue the images to the poster board with a foam brush dipped in Modge Podge. Let the images dry, and then trim the poster board even with the image.

6. Cover page 2 with an image of an apothecary lady and a lettered banner.

7. Page 3 was turned into a pocket. Glue a vintage cabinet card image to the base and add a top-hat image. The pocket was constructed with a vintage newspaper ad. Adhere the pocket sides and lower edge to the page with tacky glue. Embellish with sequins and a lettered banner. I inserted the legend of The Apothecary Lady and a lioness image in the pocket.

8. Page 4 was decorated with a vintage circus image, called Miss Leitzel, and a party hat.

9. Page 5 has a vintage circus image for the background. Add a three-dimensional image of a girl's head. Another image of a tiny girl, called

The Balloon Lady, was cut off at the waist and added along with a lettered banner. Embellish the balloon lady with a party hat made from paper, crepe-paper fringe, sequins, and glitter.

10. Page 6 was created in the same manner as page five but used The Rabbit Lady with the head of a rabbit and the body of a woman.

11. On page 7, use a vintage image for the base. Add fuchsia glitter and a lettered banner.

12. Flip the piece over to decorate page 8. Adhere a vintage circus poster image and Luna, The Star Face, in place with tacky glue; sprinkle with blue glitter.

13. Pierce a hole in the center of the left end piece of chipboard. Photocopy the circus cart pattern on page 120, and fill in the cart windows with vintage images; glue in place with tacky glue. Cover the back of the circus cart with designer paper, and then write the name of the piece on that side.

14. Embellish the circus cart with more images, rickrack, and glitter. Attach the cart to page eight with a tiny brad or wire inserted into the pierced hole. Pinch the wire in place with wire pliers.

15. Turn page 9 into a pocket with another big-top image. Glue a vintage circus-poster image as the background, and layer the big top image over the background. Create a pocket (refer to step 7 for pocket instructions). Insert a moon magician in the pocket. The moon magician was embellished with a party hat made from paper, crepe-paper fringe, sequins, rhinestones, and glitter.

16. A moveable acrobatic clown was added to page 10. Glue another vintage circus poster to the page for the background. Punch a hole in the clown image, and insert a tiny flower brad and glue the brad arms to the background with tacky glue. When the glue is dry, the clown becomes a moveable acrobat.

17. On page 11 add a big-headed ringmaster made with a vintage acrobat image. Add a vintage image of a girl's head; glue in place with tacky glue.

18. Page 12 is called the Fiji Mermaid and was also turned into a pocket. The background is another vintage circus poster. Embellish the pocket inserts with a sideshow-poster wand, Fiji mermaid, and a seahorse image. For the wand cut a piece of wire 2½" (6.4 cm) long, and use pliers to bend one end into a squiggly circle. Cut out the small poster, hot-glue it to the wire circle, and embellish with red glitter.

19. Accordion-fold two pieces of paper to make curtains for the front cover. Glue a curtain to each side of the cover. Then make curtain ties with ½" (1.3 cm) strips of paper. Glue the ties over the middle of each curtain with tacky glue; let dry. Add more vintage images and the star-dust image.

★ ★ ★

Helpful Tips and Alternatives

★ If you are unable to locate matte board backing, use foam core.

★ Cut through foam board or thin wood sheets with a heat tool and an X-acto knife.

CREATING AN ART CARD

AN ART CARD IS THE SAME
AS AN ARTIST TRADING CARD.
HERE ARE SOME BASIC
INSTRUCTIONS AND TECHNIQUES
SO YOU CAN BEGIN YOUR
ART-CARD JOURNEY.

BASIC INSTRUCTIONS

1. Glue designer papers to the 2½" x 3½"
   (6.4 x 8.9 cm) base with Modge Podge.

2. Layer your images and ephemera onto the
   base, gluing them in place with Modge Podge.

3. When the piece is dry, embellish with paints,
   glitters, and found objects of your choice.
   Glue objects in place with tacky glue.

★ ★ ★

HELPFUL TIPS
AND ALTERNATIVES

★ Make a three-dimensional frame by adding
   Model Magic to the edges of the base.

★ Turn your art cards into doll cards by gluing the
   head and torso of a doll image to the upper edge
   of the card, the arms to the sides, and legs to the
   lower edge.

★ Create a fabric or cross-stitch art card.

★ Turn your school photos into art cards.

bo·tan·i·cal (bə-tan´ĭ-kəl)
pertaining to plants and plant life
as it relates to man

MATERIALS

★ basic tool kit; see page 13

★ one 2½" x 3½" (6.4 x 8.9 cm) piece
  of chipboard, matte board, poster board,
  or a playing card

★ paper (designer, handmade, wallpaper,
  tissue, and crepe paper, etc)

★ vintage images, ephemera

★ various rubber stamps

★ glitter and glitter-paint pens

★ acrylic paints

★ glue: Modge Podge, tacky glue

★ other: rhinestones, sequins, beads,
  wire, tinsel, aluminum foil

The Fairy Opera Shadow-Box Card

After I discovered art cards I started thinking outside the box — by making art-card dolls, pockets, books, and a shadow box.

INSTRUCTIONS FOR THE FAIRY-OPERA SHADOW-BOX CARD

In this piece you will make your own fairy opera in the form of a shadow box, which is made on a chipboard base with cardstock strips for the sides.

MATERIALS

★ basic tool kit; see page 13

★ paper (designer, handmade, wallpaper, tissue paper, etc)

★ chipboard

★ ribbon

★ vintage images, ephemera

★ acrylic paint (black, white, pink, and 14-karat gold)

★ glitter and glitter-paint pens

★ glue: basic white glue, hot glue

★ other: rhinestones, charms, tags

1. Measure and cut a 2½" x 3½" (6.4 x 8.9 cm) base from chipboard.

2. Create a shadow-box frame by cutting two 1½" x 4½" (3.8 x 11.4 cm) strips and two 1½" x 3½" (3.8 x 8.9 cm) strips from cardstock. Fold under one long edge of each strip ½" (1.3 cm). Center a strip along each corresponding side of the chipboard with the ½" (1.3 cm) folded section flush with the back of the chipboard; hot-glue in place on the back of the chipboard.

3. Fold each strip to the front of the chipboard, and hot-glue the ends together to form a box shape.

4. Add a vintage image inside the box frame, and add decorative paper to cover the back. See pages 113 and 120 for image selections.

5. Embellish your shadow box with paint, ribbon, rhinestones, charms, and a variety of glitter.

Alice's Wonderland Art-Card Booklet

The first book I ever received was the classic *Alice in Wonderland* from my Aunt Noel when I was an infant. Little did I know that it would become my favorite story of all time.

1. Measure and cut two 2½" x 3½" (6.4 x 8.9 cm) bases from chipboard.

2. Cut out a 3½" x 15" (8.9 x 38.1 cm) rectangle from poster board. Precisely measure six 2½" (6.4 cm) sections along the poster board length.

3. Accordion-fold the poster board on the lines. Glue the end sections to the two pieces of chipboard with tacky glue; let dry.

4. For the cover, reduce a Victorian-scrapbook image to fit, and print two copies. Glue the images to the front and back covers.

5. Digitally enhance your own images or photocopy vintage images from *Alice in Wonderland*, or photocopy the images on page 121 to measure 2½" x 3½" (6.4 x 8.9 cm). Glue the images to the pages of your book with white glue. Embellish the pages with glitter, rhinestones, charms, and tags.

6. Roll Model Magic into a ⅓" (8 mm) -diameter rope. Use white glue to attach the rope to the front cover for a border. Form the letter "A" with the remaining rope, glue to the front cover, and paint with 14-karat-gold acrylic paint. Add a ribbon to close the book.

MISS SPELLBINDER'S MAGIC COOKBOOK

Miss Spellbinder, the legendary head mistress
of Spellbinder's Academy, is a wonderful baker
that frequently conjures up delicious sweets
and treats for her
students to enjoy!
This is a reproduction
of her famous recipe book.

Miss Pudding's Brownies

INGREDIENTS:

- 1 cup butter
- 5 eggs
- 3 cups sugar
- 1 tablespoon (
- 1-1/2 cups flo
- 1 teaspoon sa
- 2-1/2 cups ch
- 8- 1 ounce squ

PREPARATIO

Preheat oven to 375 d
Grease a 9 x 13 pan.
Melt chocolate & bu
a saucepan over low
In a mixer, beat eggs
at high speed for 10 m
Blend in chocolate, flour & salt until just mixed.
Stir in the nuts. Pour into prepared pan.

Bake for 35-40 minutes. (Don't overbake.)

Cool and frost if desired, but that is not necessary.

MATERIALS

- ★ basic tool kit; see page 13
- ★ two 6" x 8" (15.2 x 20.3 cm) unfinished wooden craft frames with glass
- ★ 10 photocopied or printed baking recipes
- ★ paper (designer, handmade, wallpaper, tissue, and crepe paper, etc)
- ★ poster board (large sheet)
- ★ ribbon
- ★ tinsel chenille stems
- ★ vintage images, ephemera
- ★ glitter and glitter-paint pens
- ★ acrylic paint (brown, light green, light purple, pink, red, cream, 14-karat gold)
- ★ acrylic antique medium: brown
- ★ tools: hand drill with ½" (1.3 cm) drill bit
- ★ glue: basic white glue, hot glue
- ★ other: rhinestones, charms, keys, ornaments, millinery flowers, tags

Instructions for Miss Spellbinder's Magic Cookbook

1. Paint the two wooden frames with a mix of light purple and pink acrylic paint. When dry, highlight the frames with 14-karat gold paint; let dry.

2. Place the frames on top of each other with the flat backs facing and edges aligned. Mark three holes on the left side of the upper frame. Mark two holes, each 1½" (3.8 cm) from the upper and lower edges. Mark the middle hole centered between the other two. Drill a hole at each mark through both frames.

3. Cut ten 5" x 7" (12.7 x17.8 cm) rectangles of poster board. Line up each page with the frames, and mark the hole locations. Punch the holes in the pages.

4. Cut three 10" (25.4 cm) strips of grosgrain ribbon. Thread a ribbon through the cover and the pages at each hole; tie closed with a knot and bow.

5. Insert an altered or vintage image into the front and back frames; embellish with hats, wings, glitter, and ribbons. Add small pockets for storing extra images, a wand, or paper doll to the back of the frames.

6. Glue your choice of recipe pages onto right-hand pages with white glue. Age the edges of the poster board pages with antique medium; let dry.

7. Decorate the recipe pages and opposing pages with vintage images, and tiny scenes reminiscent of the opera, circus, or sweet shop. See pages 120 and 122 for image options. Embellish with crepe paper, paper pinwheels, ribbons, recipe tags, keys, ornaments, and glitter.

8. To make a paper pinwheel, cut a half-dollar-size circle from cardstock. Also cut a 2" x 8½" (5.1 x 21.6 cm) strip from an 8½" x 11" (21.6 x 27.9 cm) sheet of scrapbook paper. Accordion-fold the strip, and then cut it in half lengthwise. Arch one strip to form a half circle and hot-glue it to the cardstock circle. Repeat with other strip, and then glue the strip ends together.

9. Hot-glue two ribbons to the side-opening edges of the frames. Tie the ribbons together to close the book.

"Miss Spellbinders Book
of Fairy Sweets"
By: Lady Kettell

Page One:
Eva's Chocolate Chip Cookies
Page Two:
Miss Pudding's Brownies
Page Three:
Fairylinda's Lemon Coconut Bars
Page Four:
Flora's Fairy Gingerbread Cake
Page Five:
Cherriana's Fairy Cherry Cupcakes
Page Six:
Plumina's Sugar Plum Cake
Page Seven:
Fairy Lavender Cookies
Page Eight:
Fairy French Toast
Fairy Butter
Page Nine:
Rose's Rose Petal Jam

FAIRY SWEETS

Miss Pudding's Brownies

INGREDIENTS:

• 1 cup butter
• 5 eggs
• 3 cups sugar
• 1 tablespoon vanilla
• 1-1/2 cups flour
• 1 teaspoon salt
• 2-1/2 cups chopped pecans, toasted
• 8-1 ounce squares of unsweetened chocolate

PREPARATION:

Preheat oven to 375 degrees F.
Grease a 9 x 13 pan.
Melt chocolate & butter in
a saucepan over low heat; set aside.
In a mixer, beat eggs, sugar & vanilla,
at high speed for 10 minutes.
Blend in chocolate, flour & salt until just mixed.
Stir in the nuts. Pour into prepared pan.

Bake for 35-40 minutes. (Don't overbake.)

Cool and frost if desired, but that is not necessary.

Trixie-the-Pixie's Journal

Trixie is a sweet pixie from Candywood. She loves to frolic in the garden and write and draw in her journal, telling stories of her day.

Materials

- ★ basic tool kit; see page 13
- ★ unfinished 6" x 8" (15.2 x 20.3 cm) wooden craft box with hinges and a clasp
- ★ fabric scraps
- ★ quilt batting or cotton balls
- ★ paper (designer, handmade, wallpaper, tissue, and crepe paper, etc)
- ★ brown paper bag
- ★ poster board
- ★ ribbon
- ★ tinsel chenille stems
- ★ vintage images, ephemera
- ★ Model Magic modeling material
- ★ glitter and glitter-paint pens
- ★ acrylic paint (pink, red, cream, yellow)
- ★ acrylic antique medium: brown
- ★ glue: basic white glue, Modge Podge, hot glue
- ★ other: rhinestones, charms, keys, ornaments, millinery flowers, tags

As you can see, pixies love to journal, and that is why I created this project as a tribute to Trixie—my pixie friend. Now you can create a special keepsake journal box, just like Trixie's.

INSTRUCTIONS FOR TRIXIE-THE-PIXIE'S JOURNAL

1. Paint the wooden box with two coats of pink acrylic paint. When the paint is dry, distress the box with antique medium.

2. Decorate the box cover with a vintage cabinet-card image, party hat with tinsel, paper pin-wheels, and charm embellishments sculpted from Model Magic. Gather and glue a crepe-paper border that extends from the outside edges of the box. Cover the inner crepe-paper edges with ribbons, a rhinestone buckle, lettering, and glitter.

3. Hot-glue fabric to the inside front, and back sides of the box. Fill the journal box with a handmade-paper booklet, pixie ephemera, wand, and paper-bag fairy doll.

4. To make the paper-bag doll, enlarge an image of the girl, (See page 122), to about 2" x 7" (5.1 x 17.8 cm). Cut two 3½" x 7½" (8.9 x 19.1 cm) rectangles from a plain brown paper bag. Glue the girl image to one paper bag rectangle with Modge Podge; let dry. Trim the excess paper around the image edges. Trim the remaining paper-bag rectangle to match. Hot-glue the two paper bag pieces together along the edges, leaving a 2" (5.1 cm) opening. Stuff with batting, and then glue the opening closed. Add a tinsel-chenille-strip border with hot glue, and then add glitter.

RECYCLED HARDWARE

DURING MY TRAVELS

with the art circus I met a lot of people and
collected an array of artifacts.

COME WITH ME

as I revisit this world of magic and mayhem, and
discover another world located behind the red
curtain—a place where secrets stay buried
and the unusual is common.

{ *For re-creating this world,* }

I CHOSE TO RECYCLE OBJECTS

that I had around the house such as scrap wire,
ornament caps,
a small birdcage,
floral birds,
rubber-toy animals,

{ *and more.* }

Rusty-doll Effigy

I will begin with a lady I met named Sophie Cromwell. She is a sorceress who has amazing powers and transformation skills.

I noticed she was wearing a wire skirt with items hanging from it, a pointed hat, and a corset. This doll was created as a dedication to Sophie and that day.

MATERIALS

- ★ basic tool kit; see page 13

- ★ doll form from a tassel-making kit

- ★ poster board or cardstock
  (large sheet, any color)

- ★ paper (designer, handmade, wallpaper,
  tissue paper, etc.)

- ★ fabric remnants

- ★ ribbons, trims, lace, jewelry findings,
  holiday ornaments

- ★ vintage images, ephemera

- ★ wire

- ★ Model Magic

- ★ glitter and glitter-paint pens

- ★ acrylic paint (black, brown, light blue,
  light green, pink, cream, 14-karat gold)

- ★ gesso

- ★ gel medium

- ★ letters: foam, wood, chipboard

- ★ tools: paper punch with a ⅛"
  (3 mm) point

- ★ glue: Modge Podge, tacky glue,
  industrial glue, hot glue

- ★ other: rhinestones, jump rings, metal
  pieces, ornament caps, glass bits

★ ★ ★

HELPFUL TIPS
AND ALTERNATIVES

- ☆ Buy a premade dress form online or at the
  craft store.

- ☆ Make a dress form using tinsel chenille stems
  for the look of a vintage ornament.

- ☆ If you don't have a porcelain-doll form, use
  a plastic doll, or print two copies of a vintage
  image (reverse one image), and then glue them
  to the front and back of poster board.

Instructions for Sophie's Confection

Repeat to wrap the remaining wires to the circles (refer to the image for an example). Bend over the wires extending from the top, pinch them together, insert them into the doll base, and secure with industrial glue; let dry.

3. Cover any unsightly wire bits, which connect the doll to the form, with Model Magic material. Mold the Model Magic into a short skirt that partially covers the upper portion of the wire skirt; let dry.

4. Paint the Model-Magic skirt with gold paint, and add gold glitter.

5. Glue a crown shape to the doll's head with industrial glue; let dry. Make a cone shape from designer suede paper, and then add the cone to the inside of the crown with more industrial glue.

6. Embellish the doll bodice and hat with sequin trim and rhinestones.

7. Enhance the wire skirt by tying four ribbons to the upper portion, spacing them evenly around the form. Reduce a variety of vintage images, glue them to poster board with tacky glue, and then add crepe paper and glitter. Punch a small hole near the upper edge of each image. Attach the images to the wire skirt with jump rings or thin ribbon.

1. Cut a 6", 8", and 10" (15.2 cm, 20.3 cm, and 25.4 cm) length of craft wire. Shape the wires into a small, medium, and large circle.

2. Cut four 12" (30.5 cm) lengths of wire. Wrap the wire lengths around the wire circles to shape a dress-form skirt. Wrap the beginning of a wire around the large-circle hoop three times, around the middle-size circle three times, and then around the smallest circle, keeping the circles equidistant apart and leaving a 2" (5.1 cm) wire segment extending above the smallest circle.

CARNIVAL TOYS

WHEN YOU GO TO THE CARNIVAL, THERE IS SO MUCH TO DO, AND THE BEST PART IS WINNING A PRIZE.

Fennell and James Carlisle are dedicated to creating the best experience one can have at the circus. There are many artisans employed by the Carlisles, and together they create tiny replicas of the animals in the show, such as Jeannie the Ballerina Giraffe and Alaister the Lion. Re-create these objects of magic with recycled items to give away at parties or to keep for yourself.

MATERIALS

★ basic tool kit; see page 13

★ large rubber toy lion and giraffe

★ paper (designer, handmade, wallpaper, tissue paper, etc.)

★ ribbon, sequin trim

★ package of pearls

★ tinsel chenille stems

★ Christmas tinsel ribbon, maroon

★ crepe paper, gold

★ floral wire

★ glitter and glitter-paint pens

★ acrylic paint (black, brown, light blue, light green, pink, red, yellow, white, cream, 14-karat gold)

★ glue: Modge Podge, tacky glue, hot glue

★ other: rhinestones, beads, doll hats, top hats

INSTRUCTIONS FOR JEANNIE, THE BALLERINA GIRAFFE

1. Paint a shirt on the rubber giraffe from the lower neck to the waist, and down the front legs to the knees, with two coats of light blue acrylic paint; let dry.

2. Cut a long piece of gold crepe paper about 3" (7.6 cm) -wide, and fan the paper around the waist to form a skirt; hot-glue in place.

3. Hot-glue a piece of maroon tinsel around the skirt's upper edge to cover up the glued crepe-paper edge. Hot-glue a piece of maroon tinsel around the paint edge at the front knee.

4. Paint the giraffe's lips red and her cheeks pink to makeup her face; let dry.

5. Thread a few pearls onto floral wire to form a necklace. Wrap the necklace around the giraffe, twist the ends together, and then cut off the excess wire.

6. Form a cone hat out of designer paper; hot-glue the ends in place. Hot-glue the hat to the giraffe's head. Embellish the hat with maroon tinsel, crepe-paper circles, sequins, rhinestones, glitter, and a piece of tinsel garland at the point of the hat.

Instructions for Alaister, the Lion King

1. Add cheeks to the rubber lion's face with pink acrylic paint.

2. Paint the lion's body pink from the neck to just above the feet; let dry. Use red paint to add polka dots. Attach crepe paper and blue tinsel around each leg, just above the feet.

3. Make a crown with a gold tinsel chenille strip shaped into a circle; twist the ends in place. Shape two more chenille strips into a zigzag, twisting each lower point around the circle base. Finish the crown with paper triangles cut from designer paper. Hot-glue the paper triangles to the back of each tinsel triangle. Hot-glue the crown to the lion's head.

✯ ✯ ✯

Helpful Tips and Alternatives

✯ Tea-stain your pipe cleaners to age them.

✯ Cut circles with a hole in the center from bridal tulle. Use the circles to create the giraffe's skirt instead of crepe paper.

✯ Try lightly painting crepe-paper streamers with acrylic paint, or use a rubber stamp and ink to add a pattern to the crepe paper.

DOLL OF ECLECTIC ORIGIN

During a trip to Austria, I met a woman named Mirabelle who wore a powdered wig, a fancy dress, and lots of jewels. The odd thing was the lower part of her dress was a birdcage where her pet bird, Gertie, comfortably sat. This project is dedicated to Mirabelle and Gertie.

Instructions for Mirabelle and Gertie

1. Remove some of the birdcage wires with a wire cutter to form an opening at the skirt front.

2. Sculpt a doll's bodice and head from Model Magic, and then hot-glue it to the top of the birdcage; let dry overnight to harden.

3. Paint the Model Magic with a mix of cream acrylic paint with a small amount of brown; let dry. Use paint to add facial features. When dry distress the clay form with antique medium.

4. Paint the small wooden square base, and attach the bird to the center with hot glue. Add a tinsel-chenille-strip crown to the bird's head. Insert the bird into the birdcage, and glue the wooden base to the bottom of the cage with industrial glue.

5. Create corset lacing on the doll's front torso by hot-gluing seed beads and ribbon to the form. Wrap a piece of crepe paper around the top of the birdcage; hot-glue in place. Repeat with a layer of fabric, leaving the door to the bird cage uncovered. Accordion-fold a length of wire-ribbon, and then hot-glue the ribbon to the base of the birdcage between the fabric edges.

6. Add accordion-folded paper strips to the fabric opening edges. Embellish the skirt with beaded lace, flowers, rhinestones, charms, and ribbon. Paint the fairy wings with pink and white paint, and secure to the doll's back with hot glue.

8. Form a powder wig from glue and cotton balls, hot-glue to doll's head, and then add some pearls to the hair. Make and add a pearl necklace to finish.

Materials

★ basic tool kit; see page 13

★ small wooden square block

★ wire birdcage ornament or a wire dress-form base

★ floral bird (cut off stem)

★ paper (designer, handmade, wallpaper, tissue, and crepe paper, etc)

★ fabric remnants

★ cotton balls

★ ribbons, trims, beaded lace

★ jewelry findings

★ Model Magic

★ glitter and glitter-paint pens

★ acrylic paint (black, brown, pink, white, cream)

★ acrylic antique medium: brown

★ glue: white glue, industrial glue, hot glue

★ other: rhinestones, jump rings, charms, millinery and paper flowers, tinsel chenille stems, doll fairy wings

★ ★ ★

Helpful Tips and Alternatives

✭ Buy a premade wire-bird form online or at the craft store.

✭ Make a bird from wire and paint it with acrylic paint.

THE SECRET LANTERN

HAVEN'T YOU ALWAYS DREAMED OF HAVING A MAGICAL LANTERN, WHICH COULD GUIDE YOU THROUGH FAIRYLAND?

A lantern, which would clearly lead you down the rabbit hole to Wonderland?
Now you can with this project. All you need is a lantern, paint, some paper, and images.

INSTRUCTIONS FOR A SECRET LANTERN

MATERIALS

★ basic tool kit; see page 13

★ lantern (available at discount, craft, or antique stores)

★ paper (designer, handmade, wallpaper, tissue paper, parchment, etc)

★ parchment paper

★ vintage images, ephemera

★ ribbon

★ glitter and glitter-paint pens

★ acrylic paint (brown, light green, light blue, light purple, red, pink, yellow, white, cream)

★ acrylic antique medium: brown

★ glue: basic white glue, industrial glue, wood glue

★ other: rhinestones, charms, chipboard letters, jump rings, chandelier crystal pieces

1. Carefully remove the lantern panels without breaking them. If the lantern panels are glass, protect yourself with goggles and gloves. Use wire pliers and a pick to help remove the panels.

2. Paint the lantern with wood glue; let dry. Then paint the lantern with several coats of a mixture of light blue and green acrylic paint; let dry between coats.

3. Cover one side of a lantern panel with parchment paper, and then cover the other side with designer paper, vintage image, or collage of your choice, using white glue. Repeat to cover the remaining lantern panels. Use a rolling pin or brayer to roll out any glue bubbles for a flat surface.

4. Put the lantern panels back in place. Embellish the upper portion of the lantern with paint, paper, and glitter. Add chipboard letters, and then sprinkle them with clear glitter.

5. Join several chandelier crystals with jump rings, and then attach them to the lantern for a long handle. Tie 36" (0.9 m) of ribbon into a bow around the base of the handle.

★ ★ ★

HELPFUL TIP

★ Use battery operated tea candles in your lanterns, instead of real candles.

CHAPTER SIX

THE MAGICAL GALLERY: ARTWORK AND INSPIRATION FROM CONTRIBUTING ARTISTS

★ ★ ★

ART AND ARTISTS ARE ALL AROUND US.

And we each have hidden wells of talent waiting
to be discovered and explored.

★ ★ ★

SEVERAL YEARS AGO I CREATED
The Faerie Zine

as a way to find my fellow artists, promote them, and let the world
see the magical and wonderful work being done. A few years later
and with thousands of members, I was able to do that, and
it is in this community that I derive the most inspiration.

★ ★ ★

ALLOWING YOURSELF TO CREATE
FROM THE HEART,

{ *as I do, and as do the contributing artists in the book,* }

adds the fullness of personal expression to your creative work.
Each of these artists has given me so much inspiration,
encouragement, and joy. I am honored to be a part of their world
and hope you will enjoy their exciting and imaginative creations.

No circus is complete without a ringmaster and his hat. *Ringmaster Magnifique* is made from crepe paper, a vintage family photo, glass glitter, and other embellishments.

Duo de Cirque hat is made from a vintage French circus photo, crepe paper, glass glitter, a glass ornament, and other embellishments.

LAURIE DUNCAN

HAPPY AS A LARK DESIGNS
HTTP://HAPPY-AS-A-LARK-
DESIGNS.BLOGSPOT.COM
EBAY USER ID: HAPPY-AS-A-LARK

EVIE DUNN

EMAIL EVIE AT:
EVIESENCHANTMENT@YAHOO.COM

Français, the Fairy is a romantic fairy made from vintage items including brown velvet roses, pipe cleaners, silk flowers, tulle, paper mâche, crepe paper, and glitter.

The *Fairy Birdcage* holds a captured fairy and is made from a hand-painted birdcage, fairies, feathers, paper, glitter, and other found objects.

Wanda Eash

WWW.TWOCRAFTYMULES.COM

This piece is called, *Fairy Wishes.* It is an art-block doll made from wood, a cabinet card, chalks, organza, glitter, metal, rhinestones, paper, and trim.

Circus Fun is a jewelry piece made from polymer clay, resin, rhinestones, and mica powder.

EILEEN GROBECK

HTTP://CHEESECLOTHMOON.WORDPRESS.COM

The *Circus Matchbook Dolls* were made from matchbooks, paper, images, and glitter.

Dragonfly Faerie is a magical circus pull toy made from a small box, wood wheels, paper, images, inks, and paint.

JENNIFER HAYSLIP

EYE CANDY CREATIONS,
HTTP://SWEETEYECANDYCREATIONS.
TYPEPAD.COM

AMANDA HOWARD

MAYGREEN FAIRIES,
WWW.MAYGREEN-FAIRIES.CO.UK

Here are two fantasy-themed vintage-art pieces. One, called *Flight of Fancy,* is made using altered-art techniques from paper, images, inks, and glitter.

Cupcake Fairyland is a deliciously sweet box assemblage created from a variety of found materials such as a bunny, vintage ephemera, images, rhinestones, sequins, chenille, tulle, and ribbon.

Lori Karla

HTTP://FAERIEWINDOW.BLOGSPOT.COM,
WWW.FAERIEWINDOW.ETSY.COM

All Is Sweet in the Faerie Wood is an altered-art assemblage made from a vintage cigar box, images, ephemera, ribbon, crepe paper, and other found objects.

Send in the Clowns is a whimsical piece made from papier mâché and paper-clay figures on a box decorated with designer papers, acrylic paints, and glass glitter.

SANDY KOTERBA

SOULIEKOTERBA74@YAHOO.COM

IZABELLA DEBRA PIERCE

HTTP://IZABELLA.TYPEPAD.COM

The *Circus-Box Assemblage* was made from wood, wood clay, paints, decorative papers, glitter, and wire with a variety of collage techniques.

This piece, *Mixed-Media Assemblage*, is made from a stretched artist canvas. One side is altered with images and paints, while the other is embellished with jewelry pieces.

Alejandra Pliego

Iside Arte, www.flickr.com/photos/iside.arte

Dancing Inside My Golden Jail is a beeswax collage on cardboard with added papers, acrylic paints, and gesso.

My Particular Theater is another beeswax collage on cardboard with papers, acrylic paints, and gesso.

DEBRINA PRATT

HTTP://WHIMSICALWORLDOFFAIRIES.
BLOGSPOT.COM

GINA SMITH

HTTP://LILLYSOFLONDONISH.
BLOGSPOT.COM

This is an enchanting fairy-cake piece called *Do You Want to Play?* made from plaster, roses, trim, paints, and a metal stand.

This unique piece is called *Marie Antoinette* and is a paper-mâche bust embellished with a variety of papers, feathers, and paints.

MARLA TOMLINSON

WWW.MARLASFAERYTAILS.COM

Blue Diamond is a mixed-media painting, which is also made with a variety of papers and painting techniques. This piece resembles the romance of Marie Antoinette.

The Fiji Mermaid is a mixed-media painting made from a variety of papers and painting techniques reminiscent of the circus sideshows.

GALLERY OF SHARED IMAGES

★ ★ ★

THIS GALLERY OF VINTAGE AND ALTERED IMAGES

is provided for you to use to make the projects in this book or your own altered artworks.
Make color photocopies, or scan them into your computer if you
would like to make further digital alterations. { *Enjoy!* }

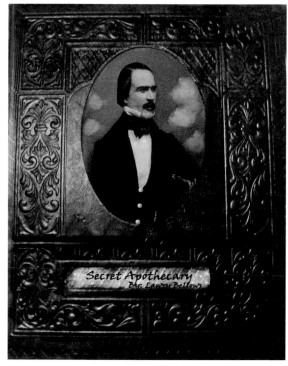

Alistair's Closet of Mystery,
Page 20

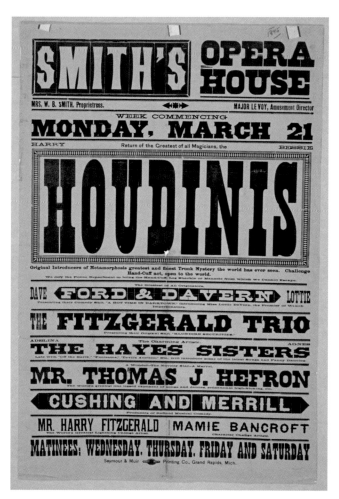

Alistair's Closet of Mystery,
Page 20

Alistair's Closet of Mystery,
Page 20

Alistair's Closet of Mystery, Page 20;
and Crystal-Ball Wands, Page 66

Alistair's Closet of Mystery,
Page 20

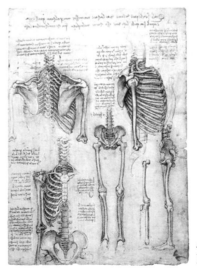

Alistair's Closet of Mystery,
Page 20

Alistair's Closet of Mystery,
Page 20

Alistair's Closet of Mystery,
Page 20

The Fairy Opera Shadow-Box Card, Page 76
and Trixie-the-Pixie's Journal, Page 84

Alistair's Closet of Mystery,
Page 20

Alistair's Closet of Mystery,
Page 20; Carnival Theatres,
Page 50; and Circusology Art-
Card Pocketbook, Page 70

Alistair's Closet of Mystery, Page
20, and Miss Spellbinder's Magic
Cookbook, Page 80

Alistair's Closet of Mystery,
Page 20

Cone-Shaped Pocket Posy,
Page 29

Cone-Shaped Pocket Posy,
Page 29

Wizard of Oz Peat-Pot Pocket Posy,
Page 30

Wizard of Oz Peat-Pot Pocket
Posy, Page 30

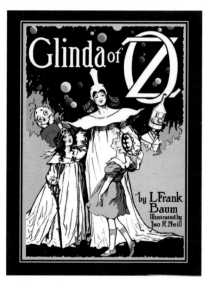

Wizard of Oz Peat-Pot Pocket
Posy, Page 30

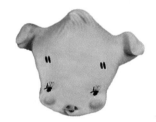

The Princess and the Pea,
Page 34

The Princess and the Pea,
Page 34

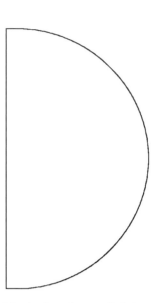

Marie Antoinette Soirée,
Page 38

Marie Antoinette Soirée,
Page 38

The Traveling Bumbelinas,
Page 46

Pixie-Pageant Crown,
Page 42

The Traveling Bumbelinas,
Page 46

Carnival Theatres,
Page 50

Carnival Theatres,
Page 50

Carnival Theatres,
Page 50

Captured Cupcake-Princess,
Page 61

Circusology Art-
Card Pocketbook,
Page 70

Circusology Art-Card Pocketbook, Page 70

Carnival Theatres, Page 50; Rusty Doll Effigy, Page 88

The Fairy-Opera Shadowbox Card, Page 74

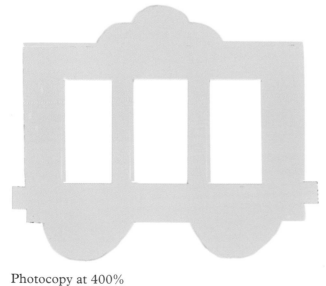

Circusology Art-Card Pocketbook,
Page 70

Miss Spellbinder's Magic Cookbook,
Page 80

Photocopy at 400%

The Mad Tea Party

The Royal Hearts Family

The Wonderland Parade

The Mad Hatter Boutique

Alice and the Flamingo

The Mad Tea Party

Mad Hatter Tea Court

Playtime in Wonderland

Alice in the Conservatory

Alice's Wonderland Art-Card Booklet,
Page 78

Trixie-the-Pixie's Journal,
Page 84

Miss Spellbinder's Magic Cookbook,
Page 80

Miss Spellbinder's Magic Cookbook,
Page 80

Artist Trading Card

Title

By

Date

Artist Trading Card

Title

By

Date

Artist Trading Card

Title

By

Date

Artist Trading Card

Title

By

Date

Suppliers of Goods

Many of the materials you will need, along with inspirational resources to make the projects in this book, are available at the following stores and websites throughout the world.

Australia

Eckersley's Art & Craft
Supplies, inspiration, and classes
www.eckersleys.com.au

South Africa

Get Crafty
Craft directory, supplies, and workshops
www.getcrafty.co.za

North America

A.C. Moore
Arts, crafts, floral, and more
www.acmoore.com

Anna Griffin, Inc.
Fine decorative paper and embellishments
www.annagriffin.com

ARTchix Studio
The ultimate source for images, tiny shrines,
art oddities, and more
www.artchixstudio.com

Autumn Leaves
Scrapbooking paper, embellishments, and books
www.creativityinc.com/autumnleaves

Avery Office Products
Tags and supplies
www.avery.com

Basic Grey
Cutting-edge designer papers, embellishments,
and more
www.basicgrey.com

Blue Moon Beads
Exceptional bead and jewelry supplies
www.creativityinc.com/bluemoonbeads

Chicks57
Wonderful gallery of vintage images and postcards
www.flickr.com/photos/chicks57/

Cosmo Cricket
Delicious designer papers and more
www.cosmocricket.com

Crayola
Coloring, craft, Model Magic, and instructions
www.crayola.com

D. Blümchen & Company
European style and vintage supplies, Dresden trims,
crepe paper, and more
www.blumchen.com

EK Success
Scrapbook papers, supplies, embellishments,
and more
www.eksuccess.com

Elmer's
Glue and other adhesives
www.elmers.com

Enchanted Mercantile
Unique collage images, vintage graphics, CD-ROM
collections, downloads
www.enchantedmercantile.com

THE FAERIE ZINE
A Zine dedicated to fantasy, mixed media, indie,
and the art world
www.faeriezine.com
http://thefaeriezine.blogspot.com

FANCIFULS, INC.
Brass charms, rubber stamps, and unique
embellishments
www.fancifulsinc.com

JO-ANN FABRIC AND CRAFT STORE
Fabric, craft, paint, and jewelry supplies
www.joann.com

KAREN FOSTER DESIGN
Designer scrapbook papers and embellishments
www.karenfosterdesign.com

K & COMPANY
Scrapbook papers, embellishments, books, and more
www.kandcompany.com

MARTHA STEWART CRAFTS
Amazing glitter, ribbon, crepe paper, packaging,
craft ideas, and more
www.marthastewartcrafts.com

MICHAEL'S ARTS, CRAFTS, AND MORE
Beads, paint, paper, floral, and more
www.michaels.com

OFFRAY RIBBON COMPANY
Ribbons and trim
www.offray.com

RANGER INK AND INNOVATIVE CRAFT PRODUCTS
Beeswax, ink, tools, and more
www.rangerink.com

STAMPINGTON AND COMPANY
Quality art and paper supplies, books, and magazines
www.stampington.com

STRATHMORE
Quality watercolor, Bristol board, and other
art papers
www.strathmoreartist.com

TALLULAH'S ART
Amazing vintage collage images and downloads
www.tallulahs.com

TINSEL TRADING
Ribbons, trims, and vintage oddities of all kinds
www.tinseltrading.com

VARIAZIONE (ZNE)
Connections for mixed-media and indie artists
www.znestore.com

VICTORIAN TRADING CO.
Unique Victorian goods
www.victoriantradingco.com

UNITED KINGDOM
Alice in Wonderland Centre
Alice Exhibition, wonderland merchandise,
and more
www.wonderland.co.uk

ALICE'S SHOP
Where Alice Liddell bought her sweets, now
an Alice theme store
www.sheepshop.com

ARTS AND CRAFTS STORE
Card and scrapbook supplies, beads, and more
www.hobbycraft.co.uk

CREATIVE CRAFTS
Supplier of art and craft materials
www.creativecrafts.co.uk

FAIRYLAND TRUST
Everything fairy, fairy queen, and more
www.fairylandtrust.org

ODDITIES ANTIQUES
Antiques, collectables, handmade items,
and supplies
www.odditiesantiques.com

PURPLE NIMBUS
Art and craft supplies
www.purplenimbus.com

THE MAGIC WAND SHOP
Purveyors of fairy and wizard wands since 1485
www.themagicwandshop.co.uk

ABOUT THE AUTHOR

EVER SINCE LISA COULD HOLD A CRAYON, she has been creating a world of fantasy. Now, in *Altered Art Circus*, she shares her unpredictable, imaginary world with you.

Lisa's various artistic mediums have been fueled by her love of history, her world travels, and her inimitable imagination. She shares her creativity in *The Faerie Zine*, a zine she founded in 2006, that is dedicated to the unlimited possibilities in the world of art and to building friendships within the artist community.

Her artwork has been published in newspapers, magazines, books, and on websites. She enjoys teaching workshops and is currently in the process of licensing a new line of products. Her imaginary world is based in New Jersey.

ACKNOWLEDGMENTS

Altered Art Circus is a book I have believed in for a very long time. It is a place I created filled with my own imagination and art—both gifts I have received from God and the heavens above. My grandmother Yolanda and Uncle Jimmy also had the gift, and I believe they are my angels looking down from above, sprinkling me with their magic and love. This book is a tribute to their artistic dreams.

My mother, Joan, has always been a huge driving force in my life—one of encouragement, strength, and love. She's been my biggest and most loyal fan, supportive in every way, and completely believes in my work and this book. Along with my stepdad, Richard, and grandfather, Anthony, who equally have watched me transform and cheered me on. And, of course, my wonderful Glenny, who fills me with ideas, lends me his undying support, and pushes me to continue. His loyalty and belief in me has added to the sparkle and magic I used in this book.

On this artistic road I gained a true identity and faith in myself. I remember the day that Mary Ann Hall emailed me. Her faith in this book, along with the staff at Quarry Books, and photographer Lexi made everything I have done worth it. And to Marla who tech-edited my manuscript—I can't thank her enough. They all have made this experience truly wonderful.

And thank you to my friends who became email buddies, lending their support when the house was a mess and my coffee cups accidentally become water vases for my paints: Vanessa, Patty, Lara, Tara, Alex, Sharon, Sue, Sandy, Evie, Tammy, Geary, Bobby, Anthony, Darrin, Tim, Pete, Paula, Theresa S., Dina, Laura, and Kelly. Also the Sally Lunn girls: Theresa, Mum, Helen, Crista, Nancy, Stacy, and Karen; my other mothers: Carrie, Rose, Sandra, and Connie; my extended families: the Egidios, Dezaos, Kaplans, Gutowskis, Ciamillos, Seniors, and the Tskiris family—Lisa and Peter Rush, Jessie, Yoli, Tommy, and Noel—for my first Wonderland book. And I can't forget the pets: DJ, Rebecca, and Ben.

Thank you to all the guest artists, and my friends at *The Faerie Zine*—your magic helps guide my day. Thank, thanks to Helga at Art Chix Studio for your generosity, The Zine Group, and all the others who have contributed to this book.

I love you Mom, Dad,
Grandma, Grandpa, and Glenny!